CLEANSE

AND

CLOSE

LAST GENERATION THEOLOGY
IN 14 POINTS

BY LARRY KIRKPATRICK

GCO
PRESS

HIGHLAND, CALIFORNIA

ACKNOWLEDGMENTS

We extend our appreciation to the many who through their means have made it possible to produce this book. The author thanks those who have helped in the shaping of content. Such a book could not come into existence without the concentrated efforts of so many converted hearts and consecrated minds.

DEDICATION

To Amanda. May she be among the victorious friends of Jesus in the last generation.

Are you ready
to cooperate with the Holy Spirit?

To walk with Jesus through the end-time?

To give the last message of grace and truth
planet earth will ever hear?

Cover design by
Anthony Schmidt

Text design and layout by
Greg Solie – Altamont Graphics

ISBN 0-9776316-0-5

TABLE OF CONTENTS

SECTION I

Weakest of the Weak Tell the Story of Jesus 7

SECTION II

Anthropology 11

   1. Born With Weaknesses and Tendencies to Evil . . . 12

   2. Lost Because of Personal Choices 22

Merit 33

   3. God Takes the Initiative 34

   4. No Merit for Our Deeds 40

Cooperation 50

   5. Christ's Character Reproduced in Us 51

   6. Obedience a Condition for Salvation 62

Incarnation 70

   7. Jesus Emptied Himself and Took Our
      Fallen Flesh 71

   8. Jesus Tempted From Without and From Within 78

Atonement 85

   9. Jesus is Currently Making the Final Atonement . . . 86

  10. Cleansing in Heaven Connected to
      Cleansing on Earth 94

Delay and Hastening 102

11. Delaying the Second Coming
    Through a Half-Gospel 103

12. Hastening the Second Coming and
    Embracing the Harvest Principle 112

Great Controversy and Decision Time 123

13. Character Witnesses to the Great Healer........ 124

14. Decision Time for Planet Earth 133

SECTION III

Invitation.................................... 142

How to Use the *LGT14*......................... 143

Last Generation Theology in 14 Points 145

Resources..................................... 151

Colophon..................................... 156

Section I

Weakest of the Weak Tell the Story of Jesus

Amanda* came into our home in April at age 4 months and left us in July, 2005. My wife Pam and I were doing foster care for the county. Amanda was a drug baby. The time she was with us coincided almost exactly with the preparation of this book. While she was with us we saw the beauty of what she was and what she could be. Her joy and smiles will never leave us.

She dropped something and we had to pick it up for her, or she would back into a corner and we had to get her out. She needed to be fed, she needed to be changed, she needed to be loved. We saw her begin to sit up, to crawl, and helped her with her first words (hi, dada, momma).

We comforted her when she cried, played with her in simple ways, sang to her, took her to church. We had to watch over her very carefully; one small object swallowed could have ended her life. She was quite dependent on us. She needed us in order to survive.

Four months later she returned to her birth father. We can never forget that day. In all probability, we will never see her again on planet earth. In all likelihood, she will never understand why we

---

*Actual name withheld.

suddenly disappeared. Probably, she will never read this book.

What does all this have to do with the cleansing of the sanctuary (Daniel 8:13, 14) or the close of probation (Revelation 22:11, 12)? What does it have to do with grasping the biblical picture of God's purposes for man in these end-times?

You see, Amanda was a methamphetamine baby. She was the weakest of the weak, born dangling by a thread from a 6,000-year-long rope of degeneracy. And yet, God will from the last generation use those like her to finish telling the story of Jesus. In the great controversy war, people like Amanda and you and I will show a world in moral collapse what the character of God is truly like. The word about God to the last generation is completely practical. It means a real solution to the sin problem. It means a way of living that impacts people, showing a side of God's love that they have never before clearly seen.

Why not just sit back until Jesus comes? Why not embrace our insignificance, sit on our hands in passivity, and wait for God to move? Why turn even one more page in this book or in the Bible? But answer that question with these:

If Jesus did it all on the cross, why are we still here? If the Reformers understood righteousness by faith perfectly, why did God raise up the Adventist Movement in the mid nineteenth-century? How will anyone know if and when God is winning the great controversy? If Jesus wanted to return a hundred years ago, why are we still here? If He settled everything in His life and death, why does God stand by and permit the horrors and sadnesses of the past 2,000 years? Was there something still unfinished after the cross? And finally, will God have to wait for a generation unborn to do what we could do but would not?

Something is left unfinished. But God is moving. Are we? Unless we are daily advancing in active Christianity, we shall not recognize the manifestations of the Holy Spirit in the latter rain. It may be falling on hearts all around us, but we shall not discern or receive it.

To us falls the task of understanding where previous generations have failed, ending in funerals rather than translation glory. What attitudes and must-be-dealt-with theological issues did they leave unresolved, still burning and crisping for us? Will our generation labor aggressively for the gospel of Christ, yet settle for the same experience that kept back previous generations to dig their graves in the wilderness?

It must not be!

There is a serious answer, and in the following pages we share the sketch. *Cleanse and Close* is by no means exhaustive. It provides only an outline. Nevertheless, we consider how the pieces fit together. In the inspired writings, God has given His people a platform, a "Last Generation

Theology" (*LGT*). You and I can be the end-products, not only of 6,000 years of decline, but of the intense ripening power of the Holy Spirit.

The heavenly sanctuary—presently—is being cleansed. The finish of Christ's intercession in heaven for us is imminent. Things are unraveling all around us. Our generation is riding the Titanic. Jesus is calling a group from every nation and kindred and tongue and people (Revelation 14:6) to live as no generation has lived before.

It is time to cleanse and close. Your generation will rise to the occasion, or sink to defeat. You will roll up your sleeves and search out God's answers, or leave the task for your children, trusting them to run the mower over your headstone at the cemetery every week until Jesus comes. The end-time battle is on.

Let's roll.

Section II

Anthropology

Under the heading of Anthropology we address Man's creation and Fall, sin and free will. Our understanding of these topics affects every other subject; it recognizes God's original purpose for man, how it has been deflected, and the pathway from our present situation to ultimate and joyous triumph.

Last Generation Theology starts with an understanding of first generation disobedience. The greatness of the trauma caused by the Fall determines how radical must be Heaven's remedy. What role does free will play? The great controversy war between good and evil hinges on this point. All subjects are wired together building on this foundation: what is the biblical understanding of man and of sin?

1. Born With Weaknesses and Tendencies to Evil

Man was designed to live, not to die; wired to succeed, not to fail. But at the Fall, his nature was dramatically disordered so that he is born with weaknesses and tendencies to evil. There is now in the fallen human organism little inclination to cause him to seek God or His righteousness.

Created for Jesus

God made all things through Jesus Christ. "For by Him were all things created, that are in heaven, and that are in earth, visible and invisible … all things were created by Him, and for Him" (Colossians 1:16). He "is not the God of the dead, but of the living" (Matthew 22:32).

When God made man, he was designed to live and flourish; not to die (Ezekiel 18:30-32; 33:11). Because he was made in the divine image, after God's likeness (Genesis 1:26, 27), he was given freedom to think and to do. He was, by his created nature, a worshipping being. He would be shown what was right and wrong; but he would not be forced to choose right. When created by and for Jesus, everything was built on the foundation of free choice.

Who is on Trial?

Lucifer, perfect in the day he was created (Ezekiel 28:15), had been granted free choice also. But he came to covet that which could never be his own: he wanted to be worshipped (Isaiah 14:12-14; Matthew 4:9; Luke 4:6, 7). He chose to serve himself; he chose the path of selfishness. He chose to dispute the Designer's design, to reject the universe's baseline principle of unselfishness. He remade himself into Satan, the adversary. Disorder and death were the result. Sin is a sort of oppression of ourselves. But not everyone is ready to follow Satan in his manic self-oppression. Whose ways are right? Whose "freedom" is actually oppression and whose "oppression," actually freedom?

God is Healer (Isaiah 53:5). He is not only man's Judge, but his Restorer. Through the prophets He went on record revealing what His character is like. Jesus, our Creator, is called "Savior," which is the translation of the Greek word that also means "Healer" (Acts 4:9, 10; 16:30, 31).

In His divine response to the sin problem He puts His dealings with man out into the open. He—God—is on trial (Revelation 14:7, 8; Romans 3:4). What is the main issue in this cosmic trial? Is He fair (Revelation 15:3; 19:1, 2). And so, a great controversy. On earth, the battleground

13

is the human heart. The conflict of the ages is fought, won or lost, in the human mind (Matthew 6:19-21; Romans 12:1, 2).

God 101

In the making of man, God created a being worthy of the hand that gave him life. His original design was for us to be holy, healthy, and happy. From the beginning we were created as moral beings; to make moral choices, to have our home in a moral universe, to echo the righteousness of a moral God. Adam and Eve were created with an original enmity toward evil.

In a moment of unwise distrust, they cast this away. From failure in the first generation, the great controversy proceeds to success in the last. God puts back enmity toward evil (Genesis 3:15). Can He do it? Can He do it without being unfair in doing it?

When God made the garden, He made it for humankind (Genesis 2:7, 8). Adam and Eve were to occupy it; Eden was to be their classroom. The course was called "God 101."

The Creator's works then testified unambiguously to the Creator's goodness. No graffiti of selfishness yet marred the grand canvas. If they trusted the Teacher, clearer and yet clearer conceptions of His character would be seen. The worshipper would emulate the unselfishness of the Worshipped. Kindergarten had begun.

The classroom had but one rule. Adam and Eve could eat from the fruit of all the trees in the garden but one. Only one tree was prohibited. They were warned that to eat of that tree would mean their death (Genesis 2:16, 17).

Death was explained to them before anything had died! They lacked any experiential reference point for death. They had to trust God. Unless He were to take away their free will and place them under compulsion, they must be responsible for their decisions. He would urge them not to disobey, but He would not prevent them from disobeying. Man either is, or is not, a free agent. God either respects the free will He granted, or He does not.

So God forbade only the eating of the fruit of the tree of knowledge of good and evil. It is hard to disobey when there is only one rule you can break! Their choice was clear: obey and live, or disobey and die.

The Fall

We know the story of their fall; how Eve went—alone—to the tempting tree. There she stood beneath the boughs of luxurious forbidden fruit, curious, wondering, dangerously alone.

Surveying the scene, she noticed a dazzling stranger in the tree. There perched this magnificent being, chomping lustily, ready to play the situation for full theatrical effect. Loud, satisfied chewing noises sounded his audible delight. Then, looking directly into Eve's eyes, he asked his carefully crafted question: "Yea, hath God said, Ye shall not eat of every tree of the garden?" (Genesis 3:1).

We've all heard the rest of the story; we've all lived with its consequences. Eve entered into discussion. The serpent flatly contradicted God. The woman was deceived (1 Timothy 2:14). She ate the fruit and ran to find her husband, leading him into disobedience. He chose to disobey God.

Adam and Eve were evicted from the garden, but granted merciful opportunity to repent. A Lamb was provided (Genesis 22:8, 13; John 1:29; Revelation 13:8). Jesus intervened. As soon as there was sin, there was a Savior. He promised He would die in man's place. He would take the penalty of the law broken, and be broken for us (1 Corinthians 11:24). He would become sin for us that we might become the righteousness of God in Him (2 Corinthians 5:21).

Their death sentence was transferred to Jesus who promised to come to earth and die on a cross. Christ agreed to become man's Guarantor and Substitute, that man, through grace, should have another trial—a second probation. The experience of Adam and Eve would stand as a warning not to distrust God's gracious will.

Impact of the Fall

What happened to man at his Fall? Originally, the members of the human race were endowed with noble powers and well-balanced minds. Their thoughts were pure, their aims holy. They were in harmony with God. The Fall changed this. Since then, all have been born with weaknesses and tendencies to evil.

Adam was changed, and every child of Adam experiences the results of the working of the great law of heredity. Today the race is weakened by the impact of thousands of years of disobedience. Like a photo-copied image itself photo-copied, and the next photo-copied from that copy, each generation of the image is degraded compared to the one before. So the members of our race, damaged at the Fall, have been decreasing in physical strength, in mental power, and in moral worth. This decrease in our powers did not occur in just one catastrophic event, but deepens with each new sinful indulgence.

Each generation is born more damaged than the one just preceding. The liabilities received in consequence of Adam's disobedience are stronger in every newborn child. Forces latent within our own disordered nature await, ready to rise from within and provoke to self-indulgence. We begin life inclined to evil.

Each set of parents bequeaths a deadly legacy of additional depravity to the humanity of the next generation. Characteristics, mental and physical, like their own, are transmitted to their children. Their dispositions and appetites affect their offspring. The children have less power to resist temptation than had the parents, and the next generation tends lower.

Our original enmity against evil vanished. Humankind was changed. Designed-for-goodness beings now found they had broken their compass.

In this light, we understand something of our desperate need for divine intervention. Though designed to reflect God's image, we have lost our gloss. The righteousness of the righteous God now evokes our resentment.

How large a crater Adam exploded for us! How relentlessly each generation sinks it deeper. Humankind has been excavating this hole for six thousand years. Adam began the digging of this awful abyss but he only turned over the first shovelfuls. And the project continues.

Splash or Cascade?

We see then two different doctrines of the Fall, the "splash" version and the "cascade" version. The "splash" version says that in one sweeping moment of disaster, the Fall came when Adam sinned.

But there have been a succession of Falls. With every sin the human race falls lower. The truth is that the Fall is much more like a cascading waterfall, gallons and gallons continuously washing over the precipice, continuously wearing the rocks below. The Fall never stopped with Adam. The Fall continued yesterday when you sinned yesterday.

What is more practical than knowing that there is no help for any of us in our fallen humanity? That, after all, God is the only One with a ladder that can reach to the bottom of this dark pit (Genesis 28:12-17; John 1:51)? That after all, Jesus is Himself that Ladder whose base rests on the earth and whose topmost round reaches to the gate of heaven?

If that Ladder had failed by a single step of reaching the earth, we would be forever lost. But Christ reaches us where we are. He took our nature and overcame, that we, through taking His nature, might overcome. He bids us by faith in His empowering grace to echo the glory of God's character. Though we are born with weaknesses and tendencies to evil, our Maker stands ready to counteract those tendencies all the way to glory (Revelation 3:21).

Conclusion

Man was created for God. As a created being he could never be an equal, but he could be made in His image; he could be a social companion for a moral God.

When the angel Lucifer rebelled he became Satan and was expelled from heaven. He did not withdraw voluntarily. God's insistence on unselfishness in all created intelligences raised the whole question of His character. Is He worthy of our worship, or has His character a darker side? Was Lucifer right in questioning God's fairness? Here is the center of the great controversy war.

When Adam and Eve disobeyed, they damaged themselves and their posterity. Each new generation sinks just a notch lower on the scale of moral possibility.

Yet, in spite of the intensive disordering of his being, man is still capable of being transformed and morally renewed. Jesus came and met us where we were, showing that we need not remain in bondage to inclinations or tendencies. He bridged the entire chasm between helpless man and accused Deity. He not only pointed out the way that leads to life (Matthew 7:13, 14), He walked the dusty trail with us.

What then are the practical helps in knowing this? The last generation needs to understand how black and deep is our sin problem. Unless we realize that there is no help for us in our disordered humanity, we will not know the depth of our need for a Savior. Unless we comprehend the destructiveness of sin, we will never grasp the beauty of God's solution of righteousness.

Because of the damage to the human genetic stream, we are born with weaknesses and tendencies to evil. We receive neither sin nor guilt nor condemnation from someone else's fall, but we are thrust into a situation where we need the healing that only Jesus the Great Physician can provide. Let us hasten to His side for strength to help in time of need (Hebrews 4:16). In our situation, that time is every hour of every day!

Discussion Questions

1. Is man, by design, a worshipping being?
2. In what way is God on trial?
3. In what situation did mankind find themselves after the Fall?
4. Did the falling stop in Eden?
5. How much help within me is there for my fallen humanity?
6. To what extent can God counteract my fallen nature in this life?
7. Which understanding of the Fall, "splash" or "cascade," says the most about the sin problem I face today?

2. Lost Because of Personal Choices

> Men and women will be lost because of personal choices, not because of being born with disordered natures.

Continental Divide

Without clarity concerning what sin is, there can be no clarity concerning what righteousness is. Without clarity on what righteousness is, we cannot know the difference between right and wrong, but are left to guess at what changes are needed in our behavior. A correct definition of sin is the continental divide (1 John 3:4). If the rivulet flows down one side of the mountain, it enters the gospel river; if the other, it becomes part of a totally different river, a false gospel.

In the Bible your prophetic heritage turns on how you interpret Daniel and Revelation. When it comes to your view of the gospel, everything hinges on how you answer the question: what is sin? Choice, or nature? Is it what we think and do, or is it what we are?

Skull and Crossbones

Let's consider lostness. Popular thinking says that we are not even lost. But if we are honest with ourselves, we admit otherwise. Random headlines from same-day news stories: in one, teenage boys killed a homeless man in Florida to "have fun" and "to have something to do." In the other, a nine year old girl stabbed to death an 11-year-old girl in New York in a dispute over a ball. No shortage of sad testimony speaks to the decreasing moral worth of humanity.

History's record screams that in us is an essential brokenness, a relentless badness, a toxic moral slime. A bloody trail of footprints bookmarks the human timeline, tracing its catalogue of atrocities. We are not, as a race, known for doing good. A skull and crossbones represents us best. Our badness is legend.

To be lost is the inevitable result of persistently misusing the freedom granted us by our Maker. Adam and Eve were free moral agents, but they abused their freedom. They allowed themselves to be overcome by appetite. In distrusting God, they sold their innocence. By their own free will they became sinners, separating themselves from the favor of God (Isaiah 59:2). It was choice in operation.

Men and Mosquitoes

God might have created man without the power to transgress His law; He might have intervened and prevented Eve from eating the forbidden fruit. But then men and women would have been automatons, mere robots. Without freedom of choice, obedience would not have

23

been voluntary. It would have been forced. There could have been no development of character. Love could not have been experienced for love cannot be forced.

Were we only a race of biological robots, intelligent creatures incapable of choice, then God's moral demands upon us would be unreasonable. His requirements would be unfair because of our inability to choose and do the right. Satan's charge that God makes unfair demands upon His children would be sustained; God's goodness would be impeached. But that is not how He is. Or, how we are.

Why do you kill the mosquito in your house? Because that insect is beyond redemption as far as its relationship with you goes. You cannot communicate with it, cannot persuade it to go against its instinctive programming, cannot compel it not to suck your blood. It is not made in the image of God; it has no capacity for moral choice.

Mosquitoes carry diseases such as malaria, filariasis, yellow fever, dengue, encephalitis, and West Nile virus. Through the transmission of such diseases, mosquitoes have caused more human deaths than any other creature. They are a health risk, a safety issue for us and our children. They are not safe to save and they cannot be made safe to save.

We are different. God made man upright (Ecclesiastes 7:29), and in His image (Genesis

1:26). He gave him noble traits of character, with no bias toward evil. But man chose disobedience and death. The result was a bent, disordered nature, inclined to evil. This, sadly, is our true estate. And yet, unlike the mosquito, we can be made safe to save!

The mosquito has bad equipment and so do we. But we were made in God's image, just a little lower than the angels (Psalm 8:5; Hebrews 2:7). The mosquito is only an insect. We have an inheritance in the moral realm.

Evil and Guilt

We inherit everything that Adam and his descendants could pass on. We inherit all of the leanings, all of the tendencies, all of the desires; thus we are born in a way that God did not originally plan. But sin comes through choice; sin, itself, is not inherited.

If we are going to understand sin as choice, then we must make a distinction between evil and guilt. Trees and animals are full of sin's results, but they are not condemned, nor are they redeemed by God, for they have no knowledge of moral values. Only man has a knowledge of moral values, and because of this knowledge he is condemned as guilty for evil acts. The atonement must deal with guilt by forgiving it and with evil results by recreating and restoring what the curse of sin has done.

Evil is in the world as an indirect byproduct of sin. When one animal kills another, we don't hold it guilty. We realize that it is only acting according to its instincts, its preprogramming. But if a human kills another human, we react differently. Why? Because we are made in God's image. We have conscience. We are moral beings. We may know and harmonize with God's will. One human being killing another usually is not only an issue of evil, but of guilt. We make a distinction between evil and guilt.

Only when we tolerate the impure thought, only when we cherish the unholy desire, is our soul contaminated (James 1:14, 15). Satan is allowed to send us unsolicited messages. He suggests and arouses thoughts and feelings that annoy even the most consecrated; but if they are not cherished, if they are repulsed as hateful, the soul is not contaminated with guilt. If light is given, but is rejected or neglected, it is then—and only then—that condemnation comes (John 3:19-21).

Sins of Ignorance

Most so-called sins of ignorance are misnamed. What are actually being described are usually sins of impulse. This kind of sin results either from a conscious choice of rebellion, or a failure to choose preventative measures—a choice to ignore the problem. Almost everything we do stems from a personal choice that we have made, even willful blindness—a choice not to know.

A true sin of ignorance occurs when we do something that is a clear violation of God's expressed will, but because of personal lack of understanding or general religious misunderstanding, we have no idea that it is wrong, and have not had opportunity to know it to be wrong. Since we cannot repent for, or even meaningfully confess something we don't know is wrong, the Bible is clear that we are not held accountable for such sins. God, in His mercy, does not condemn us (John 15:22; Acts 17:30; James 4:17). Nevertheless, we may still reap the negative consequences connected to such sins.

All sins of ignorance have been provided for in God's plan of redemption. In His suffering and death, Jesus has made atonement for all sins of ignorance. This atonement also covers all the effects of sin, such as illness, physical or mental defects, and deterioration leading to death. Neither sins of ignorance nor the effects of sin incur guilt or condemnation, and they do not require repentance, confession, or forgiveness. These responses apply only to sins for which we are guilty.

In God's mercy, He will bring to our knowledge many areas in which we have been ignorantly transgressing His law. As He enlightens our mind in these areas, we will gladly confess and forsake these previously unknown sins (Leviticus 4:14; Revelation 13:8; Psalm 139:23, 24). We will never excuse, defend, or treat lightly these sins when the light comes to us because God has been merciful in not holding us accountable before that time. When we know what is right and do not obey, guilt enters the picture. What a privilege it is when God opens our eyes and we are able to respond in wholehearted surrender, experiencing His forgiveness and gift of inward moral renewal!

At every homeward step in our experience, our repentance may deepen. We cannot be satisfied to manifest a character reflection that is only partly like Christ but still partly selfish. God will reveal to us every issue, so that at last we experience in our lives the situation of sinlessness in which Adam lived before his fall. The Lord's Prayer will have reached its mark. "Deliver us from evil," deep hidden evil that only the Holy Spirit can, and will, bring to light (Matthew 6:13).

More Guilty Than God Says?

One important question remains: does God hold me guilty or condemned for this bent, disordered nature that I am born with? Or is the sin for which I am guilty due to choices I make? How we answer this question will determine how we understand God's salvation plan. Our answer—inevitably—will be reflected in the gospel we adopt and in our personal vision of the Christian life.

Some prefer to go much farther than does Scripture. Some claim that our nature, after the Fall, itself bears guilt. Our nature, of itself, it is urged, is condemned.

Our disordered humanity has a governor. Yes, we have a faulty nature, but it still answers to the will. Our flesh, of itself, cannot act contrary to our own will. We are free to choose to disobey God. Our body is wired to our mind; our flesh can never be condemned apart from our personal choices. If we use our will to rebel, then we are choosing moral wrong. Then (and only then!) are we condemned (Ezekiel 18:20-24; John 3).

And yet, some say we are born condemned as taught by Augustine, John Calvin, and others. They say that because of our fallen humanity, even when we are not willfully sinning, our nature needs forgiveness. But the evil in my nature requires healing—not forgiveness. Sin requires forgiveness, but evil only needs to be repaired.

It is said that our nature is totally depraved. But the theory of total human depravity is wrong. It is true that there is none good, no not one (Romans 3:11). But does that describe a person who has been empowered by the Holy Spirit and who cooperates in the development of the fruits of the Spirit?

True, even then he has no righteousness that he can call his own. But it is also true that even the unconverted desire not evil but good gifts for their children (Matthew 7:11). Just as real guilt is possible through choice, so is real righteousness through chosen cooperation with God's provision and power. Our disordered human organism can pull but it cannot choose. If it cannot choose, it cannot incur guilt or condemnation.

Drug Baby Go to Jail?

We are born as if with a disease, like the drug baby. The police do not take the baby to jail for the drugs in its veins because mommy was on methamphetamines. But the baby is born into an awful situation. It doesn't need to be declared guilty or not guilty; it needs to be healed.

Guilt always has to do with one's personal choices. It makes as much sense to say man is born condemned for something he had no responsibility for, as it does to say that the victim in a head-on automobile collision, caused by a drunk driver who crossed the centerline, is guilty. No, the victim was simply in the wrong place at the wrong time—hardly a crime.

We are not born guilty, but ready to become guilty. We are not born with sin, but ready to sin. We are not born straying, but ready to go astray

(Isaiah 53:6). From the first Fall in Eden the power of evil became closely identified with our human nature, but we are condemned only for our own disobedient choices, our own sin.

Conclusion

The practical benefit of this point of *LGT* is that all dodges from responsibility and excuses for disobedience are neutralized. Personal choice makes me responsible. Sinful indulgence can and must be starved in order to make a Christian.

When we understand sin as choice, God's character is not impeached for being unjust. His gift of freedom of choice exalts the morality of His goodness and respect for His creation. He is shown to be fair in His relations and interactions with His beloved creatures. He is patient, and ready to empower us to live above the hell-bent inclinations of our nature. Praise His holy name!

Failure to so view sin results in a shallow understanding of how God relates to human free will (James 1:14, 15). If God condemns us and holds us guilty for that for which we are not responsible, then unfairness is found in His character and Satan would have been correct. But the testimony of inspiration shows that this is not the case.

It is a very practical point to understand that condemnation rises from our personal choices, not from the human organism we were born into.

The last generation needs to know that our Lord stands ready to help us choose Him. No matter your situation, no matter your unique life catastrophes, He is able to reverse self-centered habits and to keep you from falling (Jude 24).

Discussion Questions

1. How are you benefitted in having a clear understanding of sin?

2. Is our nature—disordered and inclined to badness though it is—itself guilty or condemned?

3. Who is responsible for the choices I make?

4. Can man be made safe to save?

5. What distinction do we make between evil and guilt?

6. Does evil require atonement? Does evil require forgiveness?

7. How is God shown to be fair in how He deals with men?

8. What does God's deep respect for human freedom say about His character?

Merit

Another question regarding man's salvation is whether God saves him or he saves himself. Since man is born with a disordered nature, God must start the salvation project. Man receives no merit, no credit whatsoever, for anything he does toward his own recovery. Could he somehow pay the price for his salvation, he would not be wholly indebted to God.

Some presume that if man has any active role in the salvation process, that we have introduced a righteousness by works, a salvation earned by human achievement. But James can be reconciled with Paul; faith is not the enemy of works or vice versa. The Christian must have a faith that works, and this is precisely how the gospel, rightly understood, operates for end-time Christians.

Controversy arises when believers try to sidestep God's intended achievements in the great controversy. Heaven has a very active end-time agenda, but as we labor in the gospel we mustn't drift into a salvation by works. Last Generation Theology affirms the role that God has appointed for men and women. At the same time, *LGT* recognizes that we have no ability to save ourselves. Therefore, the full integrity of the gospel is preserved.

3. God Takes the Initiative

Repentance is a gift from God, who has taken the initiative to bring it within man's reach. His grace is sent out in search of us even before we realize our need.

God Makes Repentance Possible

When Adam chose to sin, the race was damaged. It became impossible for man, in his strength alone, to overcome his now self-centered desires. The last generation must understand that repentance is a gift from God (Acts 11:18). Not even repentance can be earned; nor should it be considered human "works." When we do repent, it is only because our Father has made that repentance possible (Romans 2:4).

We score no points for our repentance. It is only our repentance because God has made it possible for us to choose it. All the strength by which we repent comes from God. He draws (John 6:44, 65; 12:32). Our part is very simple and very limited. We choose. He gives the gift.

Without divine intervention, we would never repent. Our nature is so disordered because of the Fall, that although we retain a lingering appreciation for righteousness, God must move toward us first. Only then can we turn to Him. Because we cannot repent on our own, we can never claim credit for repenting. Turning to Him is just part of being His friend.

Repentance (turning the mind around) is not a one-time ceremony or event. At every stage of our Christian experience, our repentance should deepen. But we can't even turn unless God intervenes (John 6:45). Thus, His intervention became a necessity if He would bring forth a people who would be holy, healthy, and happy.

God Himself set out to recover man. In our fallen estate, we still seek to fill the hole created by human abandonment of Him. This desire to worship is in us by design. We are constituted as worshipping beings (Colossians 1:16; Revelation 4:11). When our basic nature turned from outward to inward, there was a shift in our inclinations. Now we would seek out fulfillment in the wrong places. Our search for wholeness aims to find it in anything but in God. Thus, to remake us, He had to come after us; He had to come seeking. He came to seek and to save the lost (Luke 19:10).

He sends forth His angels and His Holy Spirit to make contact with us. He desires our recovery from the slavery of sin. He not only makes repentance possible, but is going out of His way to include us, empower us, restore us, and embrace us. He so longs to manifest His resurrection power in our lives today. He makes the impossible possible (Matthew 19:26; Mark 9:23; 10:27). Without Him we would find no repentance.

Mind-change

Repentance is more than merely being sorry for sin or its results. The Greek word speaks of a change of mind; the Hebrew, of turning. To speak of repentance merely as a deep sorrow for sin would be incorrect. Repentance is purifying and transforming or in truth it has not happened.

How much repentance is in us? Let's be clear: we do not repent on our own. God grants it—it is up to us whether we will receive it. Consider the clarity of Acts 5:29-32:

> We ought to obey God rather than men. The God of our fathers raised up Jesus, whom ye slew and hanged on a tree. Him hath God exalted with His right hand to be a Prince and a Saviour, for to give repentance to Israel, and forgiveness of sins. And we are His witnesses of these things; and so is also the Holy Ghost, whom God hath given to them that obey Him.

Christ's mission as Prince and Savior includes His giving to the people of God today the gift of a more-than-human repentance. Forgiveness and repentance belong together; actual change is understood. The legal penalty for transgression is paid through Christ; the needed heart-change is offered through Christ. He is Savior, both on the cross and in the believer.

36

Repentance includes a re-creative component in itself. The turning is not a random turning; the mind-change is not merely a change of one abstract thought for another. We are turned to God again; our mind is opened to Christ again (Psalm 51:7-12). Our Father desires to make a new Eden within.

No Self-salvation Here

Some have leveled charges that Last Generation Theology is built upon a mistaken understanding of the gospel, that it takes the emphasis off of God and places it upon man; that in *LGT*, man saves himself. Nothing could be further from the truth!

When Adam and Eve disobeyed, man was taken captive by Satan. He would have remained so indefinitely had not God specially intervened. The instant man accepted the temptations of Satan and disobeyed, Christ stood between the living and the dead. He volunteered to take our punishment and to stand in our place. Thus each human being would be granted his own personal opportunity to return to God.

Jesus made it possible for man to have a fresh start. Men and women would have a fair, informed opportunity to determine how they will align themselves morally for the rest of their existence. Only a divine intervention can create this opportunity.

God has the right to determine in what measure the lives of men and women will become

37

evidence that He has been fair in asking for their undivided allegiance. If He determines that the lives of last generation believers will aid in persuasively making His case for an unselfish universe, that is His prerogative.

The Bible is not ambiguous as to whether man earns merit by his obedience. He does not; and Genesis to Revelation so testify. Last Generation Theology does not teach a gospel wherein man earns his salvation. Who says that because God draws attention to such believers at time's end, they are necessarily earning their salvation any more than was Job when his friendship and experience were brought forth by God as evidence in the great controversy war? If God wants to point to what is happening in the lives of His friends, who are we to shout that He is doing something wrong!

Conclusion

The Good Shepherd came in the wilderness searching for His lost sheep (Luke 15:3-7). He took the initiative. Man gets another trial—one neither merited nor deserved by himself. Unfallen beings throughout the universe pay close attention to the choices of fallen humans in the great controversy war. Our decisions, our lives, mean something. They testify whom we worship, and in some measure, whether or not He is what we have claimed for Him.

The divine is reaching out; mercy is extended to unworthy man. Salvation, in the end, is all of God. Fallen man is only responding. He can claim nothing for himself (Ephesians 2:8, 9; Titus 3:5). Even his response (though not predetermined) is only made possible by the merciful God.

In summary, our good choices earn us nothing. The final generation does not save itself! Neither does it emphasize man at Christ's expense. We most decidedly affirm our fundamental dependence on our Father's gracious search for us, one of the truths standing at the core of *LGT*.

Discussion Questions

1. How do we define repentance? Does man earn it?

2. When it comes to choice, what is God's part and what is our part?

3. Does repentance include more than confession?

4. Who takes the initiative to seek to save us, God or man?

5. Why is every person granted the opportunity to choose his own moral alignment?

6. Why are the choices of our fallen race so significant to the successful resolution to the great controversy war?

7. Who is saving the final generation? God, or the last generation themselves?

39

4. No Merit for Our Deeds

Nothing we do in the Christian walk earns us even the slightest merit toward our salvation.

Salvation is About Healing and Character

In *LGT* thinking, nothing that we do earns us the slightest personal merit toward our salvation. We cannot earn heaven. We realize that our part, far from claiming any shadow of glory, is to bow before the cross and declare, "All things come of Thee, and of Thine own have we given Thee" (1 Chronicles 29:14).

The end-time Christian realizes that salvation is all about healing (Isaiah 53:4, 5; Matthew 8:17) and character (Exodus 33:18, 19; 34:5-8; 2 Peter 3:11-14; 1 John 4:8). The gospel is far removed from mere legal declarations. Down through the ages God and Satan have vied, good and evil have held center stage. Two contrasting agendas have produced their fruits. The issue in our day is not how bad people can become; by Genesis chapter six that was already settled. The question today is, what can God do when it comes to changing fallen rebels?

At time's end a generation lives and walks the earth filling Christ's design for His followers. They keep His commandments with the same faith that made Him an overcomer. The light of the kingdom shines at fullest brilliance (Revelation 3:21; 14:6-12; 1-5; 18:1). What will be the result?

So often our focus has been, "What must I do to be saved?" Having a care and concern about where one stands in relation to God is right, but some seek assurance of their personal salvation much more than they seek to deny self and copy the example of Christ. Self-centeredness is easy; focusing on God's will means walking in the Spirit. In the gospel, God is putting enmity back between man and Satan (Genesis 3:15).

very important idea.

Earning Salvation?

A clear sign of false religion is that, in some way, men earn their salvation. On the other hand, the clear sign of true religion is experiencing the faith that works (Galatians 5:6). Distinguishing between the two may at times be impossible for human observers. Only God can judge correctly.

The Protestant Reformation came to prominence in a day much different from our own. Christendom was then overwhelmingly Roman Catholic. Hence, many held to the Roman Catholic viewpoints on salvation, affirming that men are saved in part by their own works, such as indulgences, weekly confessionals, and hail Marys.

God launched the main phase of the Protestant Reformation in 1517 with Luther's protest, not against salvation by works, but against the abuse of the doctrine of indulgences. Release from the punishments of Roman Catholicism's imagined purgatory was purchased from the church and affirmed by the vendor's signature on a piece of paper. In exchange for his money, the purchaser imagined God appeased.

The Bible, of course, knows nothing of any doctrine of indulgences, or of any place called purgatory. Sins are not purged by making ourselves suffer in payment to an exacting heavenly creditor. The answer to our sin problem is not further suffering. The gospel does have, among all its aspects, a legal one; but the gospel is equally concerned with transforming man, bringing him back from sin to righteousness.

Some are ready to label anything touching the necessity of obedience as being a form of self-salvation. But God alone can read the motives; a working faith could easily appear to be a salvation-by-works plan. We must be wary of prejudging the experience of others. God alone knows if we are obedient.

We want to be changed so that God's honor takes first place (Exodus 20:3). We are determined to follow wherever the Lamb leads us (Revelation 14:4). But we are not trying to impress Him. We must not think we are to treat Him as worshippers treated their pagan gods. Our relationship with Him is secure and we are not trembling in the corner trying to determine whether He loves us. It is His good pleasure to give us the kingdom (Luke 12:32)!

The Transforming Gospel

It is not that we do nothing at all; it is that in the doing we are not earning or attempting to appease God. Make no mistake; a Christian will be doing (Ephesians 2:10; James 2:17-22). If the Holy Spirit is permitted in, life will over-flow its edges; blessing will be leaking into the world. But nothing we do in our own strength apart from God can have any part in saving us.

Some go another step, insisting that even the work that God does in us has no "saving" effect. To them, obedience can be riskier than open sin! Their "gospel" is limited to their misunder-standing of a few lines from Paul's Romans and Galatians, largely ignoring the Gospels and most of the Greek and the Hebrew Scriptures. The larger thrust of the Bible is missed.

The gospel transforms. Matthew 1:21 tells us that Jesus came to save us from sin; and informs us that not only Jesus, but Peter did, in fact, walk on the water. Mark teaches that true relationship with God comes from doing, not just hearing (Mark 3:34, 35); and that it was the faith of blind Bartimaeus that made him whole (Mark 10:46-52). Luke tells us that the prodigal needed to return before he was restored to his privileges as a son (Luke 15:20, 22, 24); and that it was while the lepers were in the very process of obeying Christ's command that they were healed (Luke 17:11-19). John states that Jesus healed the man at the Pool of Bethesda, commanding him to take up his bed and walk, and immediately he did (John 5:7-9); and that it was not Christ but the Father who did the works that appeared in Jesus' life while on earth (John 14:10).

Paul shows the same transforming gospel; the only one he knows! So he tells us that it is the power of God unto salvation (Romans 1:16); that not the hearers of the law, but the doers of it, shall be made righteous (Romans 2:13); that Jesus overcame sin in our flesh so that the righteousness of the law might be fulfilled in us (Romans 8:3, 4); that salvation means a renewing of our minds (Romans 12:1, 2); that our hope of overcoming comes only through Christ in us, the hope of glory (Colossians 1:27); and that while we are not saved by our own effort, what does save us is "the washing of regeneration and renewing of the Holy Ghost" (Titus 3:5). All the way through, it is a transforming gospel.

—> very import passage!

Character Surrender, Character Maturity

Paul urges us boldly to "go on unto perfection" (Hebrews 6:1). Some worry about the idea of perfection. But Jesus does not leave us where we are,

He lifts us up to heavenly places (Ephesians 2:6). It is His plan to stand on Mount Zion at time's end with a people who have walked with Him until there is no guile in their hearts, who at last stand transformed, without fault before the throne of God (Revelation 14:1, 5). Another word we can use here is "maturity."

God is a Perfecter. When we respond to His plea to turn to Him, He accepts us where we are and then journeys with us. We can only be faithful by going where He is leading. And He is leading us to the place where we all come "unto a perfect man, unto the measure of the stature of the fullness of Christ" (Ephesians 4:13).

We want to keep clear in our minds two different kinds of perfection: character surrender and character maturity. Perfection of character is attained and maintained throughout our Christian lives if we persist in character surrender. Whatever light Heaven is shining on us at a given time, we want to be wholehearted in our response. The only condition for salvation, really, is character surrender. We live up to all the light granted us; we turn to God at every occasion of testing; we surrender to Him every idol just as He reveals it to us. Thus we may be perfect at every stage of growth. One auto-maker strains to line-up with its chosen motto, "The relentless pursuit of perfection." In the pursuit of eternal values, we must be no less diligent.

45

Untangling Perfection and Perfectionism

Perfection is never absolute, either now or after the coming of Christ. Perfection is never equality with Christ. Perfection means neither lack of weakness nor absence of mental or physical mistakes. No one who is perfect will ever feel he is perfect. → what is perfection !?

Perfection is an unbroken exercise of faith which keeps the soul pure from every stain of sin or disloyalty to God. Perfection refers to the dynamic, growing lifestyle of the person who reflects the life of Jesus. He no longer yields to rebel, sinful desires.

Perfectionism emphasizes an absolute point beyond which there can be no further development. Originating in Greek philosophy rather than the Bible, perfectionism focuses on a quality in man which can exist independently of the abiding Christ. Perfectionism is wrong and dangerous, but so is the doctrine of imperfection, which allows the sinfulness and helplessness of man to overshadow what God promised to do for repentant sinners through the empowering presence of the Holy Spirit. To settle for the doctrine of imperfection is to plan to dishonor Christ.

Committed to the Vindication of God's Character

As an *LGT* Christian, I am not interested in my own salvation or even the salvation of others first; I am committed to the vindication of God's character. That is where we speak of character maturity. It is matured character that vindicates Him.

At the end of time comes a message. Earth travels from Eden to Eden. In the middle, a period of confusion, chaos, spurious claims, God and Satan sparring. In the end, a people are developed. Just as God asked Satan, "Have you considered My servant Job?" (Job 1:8; 2:3), so, at the close, He asks again, have you seen My servants in the end-time? Have you seen what happens when all the light of the gospel shines with all the power of the Holy Spirit on a generation that gives all of their hearts to Jesus?

At the last generation God asks the waiting universe, have you seen what living in connection with Jesus produces? Today He is readying to announce, "Here are they that keep the commandments of God, and the faith of Jesus" (Revelation 14:12)!

We are saved apart from the law (Romans 3:28), but we are not saved without law. The Holy Spirit uses the law to convict us of sin, of what is right, and what is just (John 16:8-10). The law cannot give life (Galatians 3:21), but the law is holy, just, and good (Romans 7:12). Jesus' death on the cross, far from abolishing law, upheld it (Matthew 5:17, 18). Remember, His law is a concise character sketch of Himself; it tells what God

47

is like. Can He then, by dying in demonstration of His self-givingness, annul His self-givingness? Does He, by being what He is in character, thereby destroy that same character? O absurdity!

Conclusion

While we obey because He is in us, we do not by obedience earn our salvation. The last generation Christian understands that when he has done that which his Master asked, he remains an unprofitable servant still (Luke 17:7-10). God will not give His glory to another (Isaiah 48:11). The end-time believer realizes that he has earned nothing, but his Savior Jesus Christ, through His merits, has made possible everything.

Character surrender permeates the Christian experience. Character maturity is the goal of this experience. It is the matured Christian character that provides the best evidence testifying to God's righteousness and unselfishness. The Christian may speak of character perfection but must avoid the ditch of perfectionism. The power of God unto salvation is the gospel.

Discussion Questions

1. Do we—in any way—earn our salvation? *No.*

2. If the Spirit of God is in us, will there be good works? *Yes!*

3. God accepts us where we are, but then what?
   transform us.

48

4. What, ultimately, is the only condition for salvation? *faith & obedience by love/deeds*

5. Is the work that God does in us a part of salvation? *the gospel is a transforming work*

6. What question should be more important to us than even our own salvation? *Vindication of His character*

7. What is the difference between perfection and perfectionism? *perfection = a exp. of faith, a growing exp. — perfectionism = is not biblical*

8. How does character maturation help resolve the great controversy war? *Rev. 14:12*

Cooperation

To include active cooperation in the gospel, according to some, is either legalism or Roman Catholicism. For them, obeying has become a byword. Things are fine so long as behavior is understood to not truly matter in our relationship with Jesus. James warned against such views, but from the time of Luther onward, many have treated the Greek Scriptures' book of James, and its positive references to works, with indifference at best; more often, contempt.

In our previous pages, we have seen that God will make the last generation holy. They can't get there on their own. So how? They cooperate with God. They permit Him to work in them. We call God's work in us "sanctification." Sanctification is part of the gospel. Salvation without sanctification would be an oxymoron. God will, as part of His gospel, sanctify the last generation.

Satan bitterly opposes every effort to keep justification and sanctification in a right relation to each other. But the final generation will understand and experience the full gospel, not a limited gospel. When the righteousness by faith of Scripture is operating in the life, God will finish what He has begun (Philippians 1:6).

5. Christ's Character Reproduced in Us

Justification is God's way of simultaneously counting men right and making them so. In declaring a man just, God writes no fiction. The disciple's walk continues, and through the process of sanctification, the character of Christ is perfectly reproduced in us. Both justification and sanctification are the work of God and are necessary and causative for salvation.

Title and Fitness

Salvation existing only on paper is of no use. A saved person must have his title, but it can only be known in the end whether he has his title clear if, along with the writing on paper, there is also evidence of what the title promises—a fitness in the heart (Revelation 3:4). When a man comes to Christ and accepts Him as personal Savior, he is counted as if he had never sinned. Accepting means more than mouthing words and promises. Accepting means receiving the work of God and permitting His power to re-create in his life.

There are conditions to our receiving justification, sanctification, and the righteousness of Christ. While good works will not save even one soul, it is impossible for even one soul to be saved without a faith that works (James 2:14-26).

God transforms us according to a principle that we must ask if we would receive, seek if we would find, and knock if we would have the door opened to us (Matthew 7:7, 8).

When God justifies a man, declaring him right, He also makes that man right (Luke 18:9-14). He is not granted instant maturity, but his surrender is accepted right where he is. God changes him. A mighty advance is made entirely by God's power. Justification imputes or counts man right, even as justification imparts to man rightness. All the human agent does is surrender, agreeing, "Lord, I have made a miserable failure on my own. Please take me where I am and take me as fast as I can go, the way I need to go." This is his prayer. God then takes that person and works in him according to the measure of his present spiritual capacities.

Continuous Growth

The new blade of grass is a half-inch tall, but perfect for a new blade of grass. Another is larger, has been watered longer, and is perfect for its degree of maturity. Another is full grown, has sent its roots down deeply, and stretches, green and perfect in the gentle breeze. Each is perfect for its stage of development.

All this is the same for the Christian. It is an illustration of the growth involved in our sanctification; our being made holy. The thief on the cross (Luke 23:42) was not converted for very long, and had but little opportunity after his conversion to live the new life. But for his stage of Christian growth, he was perfect. So the 80-year-old woman, who has read her Bible and shaped her life by it for most of those four-score years continually surrendering all to Christ, is perfect.

Being perfect at each level of maturity requires our total surrender. At every step in our walk with God we want to learn and meet His will. So we will be praying; we will be studying the inspired writings; we will be in attendance at the meetings of the church. We will be relentlessly pursuing our own personal devotional life.

As God reveals more of His will to us we surrender to it completely. We continue to grow. We walk into the light of truth as fast as light opens up. We say "Yes" to light—not "No"! Saying "No" is the rebel's response.

Sanctification Produces Evidence

Perhaps my neighbors tell me they are exceptional landscapers and gardeners. But when I walk out to my car I cannot avoid seeing the lawns that need mowing, the brown, dead patches of turf, the weeds and the garbage in yards. Nor can I hide what my own yard truly is. But one neighbor has a green lawn, flowers blooming, and neatly trimmed shrubs; his yard is different. I am not concerned about his claims, for I can plainly see that his yard is different from those of his neighbors. And so we have an illustration of sanctification enacted in the real world.

Entire conformity to the will of our Heavenly Father, as step by step it unfolds to us, is sanctification. The will of God is expressed in His holy law. The keeping of all the commandments of God is sanctification. Living so that we are obedient children in relation to God's Word is sanctification. The universe is watching and waiting for our sanctification (Romans 8:18-22).

In simple terms sanctification is a process of growth in one's personal holiness. Its attainment comes only as one cooperates with God and allows himself to be changed by the presence and power of the Holy Spirit.

Does following Jesus clean-up our lives, inwardly and outwardly, or is it just another high-sounding claim? Is God's way best, or Satan's? This is why we are still here. God is settling this question once and for all.

One Gospel

Justification and sanctification are part of one gospel, both counting and making right—changing rebels into the willingly obedient. A person once justified is not necessarily irrevocably saved. God can be just and justify the sinner through the merits of Christ, but no person can cover his soul with the garments of Christ's righteousness while practicing known sins or neglecting known duties. We must make an entire surrender of the heart before justification can take place; and in order for us to retain justification, we must live in continual obedience. Our lives must manifest active, living faith, working by love and purifying the soul (Galatians 5:6).

Too easily we become confused concerning our salvation. A kind of self-confidence prepares the way for a fall. We begin to think we are saved and gradually come to trust in the assertion rather than the power. Is it ever safe, this side of heaven, to feel that we are secure against temptation? Let us beware of even saying it. No Christian is beyond the reach of temptation. God's Word declares, "Many shall be purified, and made white, and tried" (Daniel 12:10). Only he who endures the trial receives the crown of life (James 1:12).

When sanctification is removed from the gospel, the truth is misrepresented. This misunderstanding causes the gospel soon to be viewed as a mere fiction of celestial accounting. Obedience is relabeled as merely the fruit of a salvation already wrought by Jesus on the cross. If salvation is only about how we are counted, and not about transformation, sanctification is made unnecessary. The purpose of the gospel is the restoration of God's image in men and women. Thus, we must have both the title and the fitness for heaven

(Matthew 22:1-14). Salvation means an entire transformation. We must be changed.

Of course, we cannot earn our own salvation; that is agreed. But today there are found many who advocate the removal of sanctification from one's concept of the gospel. Their claim is that classifying sanctification as only the fruit of the gospel strengthens the idea that we cannot earn our salvation. But taking sanctification out of the gospel takes away its strong purpose. Can God be just and Justifier? That is the Bible question (Romans 3:26). The true gospel will count right, but also actually make believers holy. After all, who really is only interested in one part of the good news?

Obedience Both Necessary and Causative for Salvation

To say that something is causative for salvation means that without it, salvation is not caused. You must have it or you are not experiencing salvation. It may be fashionable to say we are saved by justification alone, but what people mean by it rarely is biblical. Sanctification, making holy, is necessary. Without holiness, we cannot see God and meet Him in peace (Hebrews 12:14). We need the inward washing (Titus 3:5). Pure hearts shall see God (Matthew 5:8). Guileless hearts pass through the end-time and remain blameless before God's throne (Revelation 14:4, 5).

Disobedience can be forgiven; the pardon is a gift. But obedience, holiness, Christlikeness is developed—not a fact declared to be so when it is not. At the end it will not be asked of us, "What did you believe?" but the judgment will be centered on, "What did you do?" What we have done will testify to what we have become (Matthew 25:31-46). The angels will see just what kind of neighbors our Father proposes to move into the heavenly city.

Cooperation with His plans for us will have changed us from representatives of selfishness to representatives of unselfishness. Salvation means actual change, and actual change means learning to echo Jesus even while our own disordered humanity and our own defective characters war within us in rebellion toward goodness. Only obedience results in change. "Whoso keepeth His word, in him verily is the love of God perfected: hereby know we that we are in Him. He that saith he abideth in Him ought himself also so to walk, even as He walked" (1 John 2:5, 6).

When We Fail

God knows that we are but fragile creatures, that the outlook from our sin-stained lives scatters any hope. If we see with only our shamed rebel eyes, the future bodes only ultimate spiritual failure.

We want to give ourselves to Him, but we are weak in moral power. It seems as though we are controlled by our habits of sin. Our promises and resolutions are like ropes of sand. Controlling our thoughts, impulses, affections, appears an overwhelming, even impossible goal. Our knowledge of our broken promises weakens our confidence in our own sincerity. We begin to feel that God cannot accept us. We lay fallen, tears mingled in the miry mud, finding ourselves yet again in need of repentance. Is there any hope?

When we have sinned, and we need to repent again, we must lay hold of Christ with renewed determination. Opportunity still lingers. The Healer is still ready to heal. In His earthly ministry, how many did Christ turn away? Not one! Not one who sought Him was left to perish. Will He do less for us since He has embarked on His heavenly ministry?

We need to understand what the Holy Spirit seeks to accomplish through our will. An entire change can be, must be, made. It is His good pleasure to give us the kingdom (Luke 12:32). Jesus desires that we stop sinning, but when we do fail we are reminded that in Him we have an Advocate with the Father (1 John 2:1). In Him we have a High Priest who is touched with the feeling of our infirmities, who knows by experience the battle fought in our kind of flesh (Hebrews 2:18). Only by coming to Him again and again and again, only by persisting in our personal fight of faith, will we see Him in glory.

Just when we least feel like praying, that is when we must, in spite of ourselves, pray. Just when it seems hopeless, we must seek He who alone can revive that hope. Just when we are at the verge of unbelief, we must pray, "Lord, I believe! Help Thou mine unbelief!" (Mark 9:24).

When hope seems to fail and despair seizes us, we must learn to trust, to depend solely upon the merits of the atonement, and in all our helpless unworthiness cast ourselves upon the merits of the crucified and risen Savior. We shall never perish while we do this—never! When light shines on our pathway, it is no great thing to be strong in the strength of grace. But to wait patiently in hope when clouds envelop us and all is dark requires faith and submission and our will to be swallowed up in the will of God. We are discouraged too quickly, and earnestly cry for the trial to be removed from us, when we should plead for patience to endure and grace to overcome.

Let us make each occasion of failure the first step in climbing the mount of blessing again. From the lowlands, our life seems to be only failure, but later, from the vantage point of final victory, we will see our experience from a different aspect. What looked like a string of failures will then be seen as a succession of victories. By no means should we linger in sin so "that grace may abound" (Romans 6:1). But when we have denied our Lord, when we come to ourselves (Luke 15:17), let us approach again the throne of grace where waits victory through power from above (Hebrews 4:14-16).

Conclusion

Can God be just and count a man, who is not right, as right? No! And that was never His plan anyway. His great desire is to heal people, to help them become inwardly right.

The wrong understanding concerning what God does for sinners misrepresents Him. He is right and the Maker of right people. Justification counts right even as it makes right. Imparted righteousness and sanctification is the same thing. Being made holy is part of salvation. The gospel must do these things in us, for they are both necessary and causative for salvation as much as Christ's sacrifice for us on the cross. All merit for our salvation comes from Christ, whether imputed or imparted.

Though often we have tended to fall in our Christian walk, we must not abandon hope. Christ is willing to forgive and heal us. He never turns anyone away who honestly seeks Him. Jesus can turn failure into faith, despair into hope, and defeat into victory. The choice is ours!

In the last generation it is demonstrated not what God can do; He is all-powerful. Rather, it is demonstrated what God and willing believers can do together. We can become like Jesus. Or we can't. And the universe will know from our lives which is true.

Discussion Questions

1. What are the conditions for receiving justification, sanctification, and the righteousness of Christ?
2. Are asking, seeking, and knocking passive or active?
3. Is justification imputed?
4. In what way is justification imparted?
5. What is sanctification?
6. What question is God settling once and for all?
7. What is necessary in order for us to retain justification?
8. Can sanctification be removed from the gospel and the gospel remain true to its purpose?
9. Does God give up on us when we fail?

6. Obedience a Condition for Salvation

Obedience is both a condition for salvation and an ongoing requirement of salvation.

Faith and Action

Many have been subtly lured to believe that we are saved apart from obedience and that obedience is merely a fruitage of having been saved. The spiritual decline of our age is shown in the popular desire, even within the church, to have all the benefits God offers but with none of His conditions—conditions that help heal our sin problem. The common attitudes today are, "Make us well, Doctor Jesus, but we won't take Your medicine," or "But Doctor Jesus, we're not sick."

Is that really what the Bible teaches? That we aren't even sick, or that there are no conditions to salvation? This is more true: when we act in faith spiritual desires become actual facts. Faith is both a condition for salvation and an ongoing requirement of salvation. To war against obedience is to war against faith.

When Jesus met the withered man at the pool of Bethesda, He urged him, "Rise, take up your bed, and walk" (John 5:8). The man might have paused to argue with Christ that for him to make such an effort would be legalistic. But he believed Christ's word, believed that he was made whole, and he made the effort at once; he willed to walk, and he did walk. He acted on the word of Christ, and God gave the power. He was made whole.

Solving the Sequence Dilemma

Unfortunately, most of our English Bibles translate the Greek word for "faith" as "belief" or "believe." Faith is more than mental belief. The faith of the Greek Testament includes trust and willingness to obey the Person whom one trusts.

Thus, in the Bible, believing, trusting, and obeying are the same. The Scriptures insist that the Holy Spirit is given "to them that obey Him" (Acts 5:32). Clearly, we have to obey in order to receive the Holy Spirit. Yet, without Jesus "ye can do nothing" (John 15:5). So I must have the Holy Spirit to obey, but I cannot obey without Jesus. Without Jesus I cannot have the Holy Spirit. How is this dilemma solved?

What if God grants the gift of salvation first, and then obedience comes only as its fruit? Obedience is indeed a fruit of salvation, but not only a fruit. Obedience is part of the faith that says "Yes" to the gospel. Obedience is present, inescapably, at the beginning of the Christian experience. We must obey the gospel (2 Thessalonians 1:8; 1 Peter 4:17). We must have a faith that works (Galatians 5:6).

Jesus called on the rich young ruler to sell all that he had, give the proceeds to the poor, and only then to come and follow Him (Matthew 19:16-30; Mark 10:17-31; Luke 18:18-30). He saw the man was committed more to his own set of values than the values of the kingdom. He could not serve two masters, two sets of values. He must obey at the first moment of discipleship even as at each following step, or he would be no disciple of Christ (Luke 16:13; Galatians 1:10). Obedience as mere following fruit only, is a midday mirage.

But what if, in seeking a solution to the sequence dilemma, we try a different tack, saying that first we must obey in our own power, and that only then we qualify for salvation? That first we must obey, and then after we have obeyed, we receive the Holy Spirit? The problem here is that a legal religion is created. I, in some measure, have obeyed without Christ. By my obedience I have, in some measure, earned my salvation.

But there is a third possibility. Namely, that in the same—the very same—moment that we sincerely repent and ask for strength to obey, God sends us the power to obey; there is no waiting. At the same time we respond in faith, God speaks and gives us power to be obedient. Power is given us to act in obedience. In our very plea for help, He grants help. God and man speak at the same time, univocally.

In this view, obeying is neither first nor last. All God's biddings are enablings. We are not asked to do righteousness apart from His gift of righteousness. We need not wait for a stack of heavenly paperwork to be processed. Rather, in the very moment God calls for our obedience, in that very same moment He is ready to enable us. In that very same moment righteousness is imputed and imparted.

We cannot possibly keep the commandments of God without the regenerating grace of Christ. Do we realize how ready He is to empower? To re-create? He is seeking us, desiring to make us conduits for faith! He does not save us by law; neither will He save us in disobedience to law. Neither faith nor obedience saves, but neither does salvation come without the obedience of faith. Without the faith that obeys, authentic Christianity is impossible.

Kinds of Conditions

It is helpful for us to recognize the difference between what logicians call "sufficient" and "necessary" conditions. A necessary condition must be met to obtain the desired effect. There may be several necessary conditions. The operation of an automobile requires the presence of gasoline, coolant, brake fluid, a battery with an electrical charge, and a key to trigger ignition, among other things. To start the vehicle and then continue to operate it, several elements are necessary.

A sufficient condition automatically leads to a desired effect. In itself it accomplishes everything needed. It is sufficient. Put very simply, obedience is a necessary condition for one to be saved, but it is not a sufficient condition. This is because there are both objective (external to us) and subjective (internal to us) elements in the salvation process.

I must be obedient in order to be saved, but my obedience is not in itself sufficient to save me. Jesus died for me on the cross, and He made a sacrifice of sufficient value to save me, but I must actively embrace His sacrifice. The question of salvation is not alone about the sufficiency of the sacrifice but also about my willingness to embrace it.

Salvation in Two Parts

God designed the salvation plan with two parts. The objective element is entirely outside of us: Jesus lived and died in our place. The subjective element is entirely within us: we must choose to accept all that is meant by His life and death. All the merit toward my salvation comes through Jesus. His merit is valuable enough to save. But that is only the objective portion of a two-part plan. My obedience is also necessary. In itself it is insufficient to save me. It is a non-meritorious condition, a necessary but insufficient condition.

Because salvation involves external and internal factors, the objective and the subjective elements are both crucial. God makes choices; I make choices. The role of human free will is as important in the end-time as it was in the Garden of Eden. Without God I have no salvation. At the cross He provided a life sacrificed in my place.

Christ's life is of enough value, on one hand, to prove God's fairness in His dealing with sinners. On the other, Jesus shows the universe the final end of rebellion—the "wages of sin." All those who make Him their Lord and Redeemer will be saved from the Godforsakenness that He experienced.

Thus Christianity is more than the matter of God's choices. The choices of the redeemed are also important. Our Father makes it possible for us to choose Him, but we still choose. If you take human choice out of the gospel, the good news becomes merely a divine edict, an enforcement of the divine will. Grace becomes irresistible. But if grace is irresistible then there is no free will.

The Bible tells a different story. Our Father's mighty endeavors to save us are not wrought in isolation from us. He places life and death before us and then urges that we choose life (Deuteronomy 30:19). And waits. What will we do?

Conclusion

I must accept the fact that Jesus lived and died for me, or I have no salvation. Further, I must obey Him, or I have no salvation. Both are necessary. Because I can never bring any of my own works to Him as meritorious (Isaiah 64:6; Ephesians 2:9), He must die in my place and live in my life (Romans 5:8; 8:34; 1 Corinthians 5:7; 15:3; Galatians 2:20; 3:13; Colossians 1:27).

Because He refuses to override free choice, I must choose His kingdom. Because I have no power to choose I must have His help even to choose. All these I need or I have nothing.

Our obedience is a non-meritorious condition for salvation at the beginning and all along the way. We learn to walk with Jesus, following Him wherever He goes. God and man speak together in the same moment; it is the wedding of grace and faith.

For the *LGT* Christian, this is very practical. I learn day by day, moment by moment, to walk with Jesus. It is life by faith. My relationship with God deepens and so does my repentance. I must have a close walk with Christ now, for character development takes time. Jesus does not whisk us to heaven instantly when we accept Him (John 17:11, 14, 15). We continue walking here. From heaven He sends us power to obey (Hebrews 4:14-16). Jesus is more than ready to save!

Discussion Questions

1. What is necessary in order for our spiritual desires to be realized?

2. What kind of faith must we have?

3. What is wrong with the idea that first we are saved and that only afterwards do we obey?

4. What is wrong with the idea that first we must obey and that only afterwards are we saved?

5. How does the Bible solve the sequence dilemma? What does God do in the very same moment that we ask?

6. What is the difference between a necessary and a sufficient condition?

7. What is needed for a mature Christian character to be developed? How is that significant with reference to procrastination?

Incarnation

J esus did more than sit in a chair on the other side of His universe and declare us saved or lost. He rolled up His sleeves, came here where we were drowning, and dove into the situation of fallen humanity with us. At the center of Last Generation Theology stands Jesus, who took our fallen flesh and in it defeated sin. Throughout His life He was pulled toward selfishness, not by His character but because of the inwrought liabilities of the fallen human organism. Nevertheless, He overcame.

Obviously, everything in one's theology is wired to the kind of Jesus we believe in. Was He tempted only from the outside, or like ourselves, from the inside, too? Yes, from the inside as well. We say both with no shame, for He never chose the evil and always chose the good. Because He did, we know that the same kind of connection He experienced with the Father can be ours.

The nature of Christ's humanity impacts the whole redemption program. Substitute and Example, Jesus humbled Himself in an incredible descent to make possible an incredible ascent. He is the Ladder; heaven and earth are connected again. This wonderful, Christ-centered truth lays the foundation for a positive faith.

7. Jesus Emptied Himself and Took Our Fallen Flesh

During His earthly sojourn, Jesus, God from eternity and still God, laid aside out of His possession certain of His powers of deity and lived as a man in fallen flesh among men in fallen flesh. He came not to our world to give the obedience of a lesser God to a greater, but as a man to obey God's Holy Law. He could have recovered those powers at any time, but for our sakes chose to live as we do.

Christs, True and False

At the very center of Christianity is Jesus Christ. We believe on Him for salvation. "No other name is given under heaven" by which we must be saved but the name of Jesus (Acts 4:10, 12). Predictably, Satan's energies are deployed to prevent us from rightly understanding who Jesus is and how His work interacts with us.

At the center of Christ's work for man is the incarnation: Jesus leaving His divine existence in heaven to take a human body and be born into this world an infant, growing to adulthood, living a life unsullied by sin, voluntarily sacrificing that life for us, in our place, at the cross.

Religious systems have portrayed Jesus in any number of ways. One system has Him so far away, so much higher than us, that other inter-mediaries (such as His mother Mary and "the saints") are introduced to bridge the gap between Him and the rest of us garden-variety humans. Again, He is presented as the mystical Christ, inscrutable wise man, ascended master, evolved human, or upstart revolutionary. Others say He was just a man, created like ourselves; He had a beginning, but God took Him and adopted Him to a special role as His "Son." No wonder then Paul warns us against those who would come with threefold error: teaching another gospel, influencing by another spirit, teaching another kind of Christ (2 Corinthians 11:4).

Jesus Emptied Himself

The Bible tells us that Jesus was in the beginning with God the Father (John 1:1-3). He was God from eternity and never stopped being God (Philippians 2:6; Hebrews 1:8). But He took our flesh (John 1:14)—precisely how, we are not told. Precisely what, however, is clear.

Jesus, without whom nothing was made that was made, voluntarily stepped down into His creation. It was like a three dimensional Artist reducing Himself into His two-dimensional painting. Jesus emptied Himself of certain of His divine powers in order to pitch His tent side by side with our own, in conditions identical to our own. He came to earth this way, not to render the obedience of a lesser God to a greater God, but as a man to obey God's law.

The Bible commands us to have the mind of Christ: "Let this mind be in you, which was also in Christ Jesus: Who, being in the form of God, thought it not robbery to be equal with God: But made Himself of no reputation [literally, "emptied Himself"], and took upon Him the form of a servant, and was made in the likeness of men: And being found in fashion as a man, He humbled Himself, and became obedient unto death, even the death of the cross" (Philippians 2:5-8).

This was why Jesus had to parallel our situation. We are to live our life surrendered to the Father just as did Jesus (1 John 3:1-3; Luke 22:42). If He used His powers of deity to have special shortcuts for obeying that we cannot have, then He would not have shown us how to obey. So He "emptied Himself," laying aside powers that we cannot have, so that He obeyed by faith just as we must obey.

Like Every Child of Adam

It would have been an almost infinite humiliation for the Son of God to take man's nature, even when Adam stood in his innocence in Eden. But Jesus accepted humanity when the race had been weakened by four thousand years of sin. Like every child of Adam He accepted the results of the working of the great law of heredity. What these results were is shown in the history of His earthly ancestors. He came with such a heredity to share our sorrows and temptations, and to give us the example of a sinless life.

He trusted in the Father as is the privilege of every child of Adam. He exercised faith. When Satan came to tempt Him, he found no foothold (John 14:30). There was in Jesus nothing that responded to Satan's sophistry. He did not consent to sin. Not even by a thought did He yield to temptation. And here is the good news: so it may be with us (Psalm 17:3; Revelation 3:21)! Jesus lived as a man just as we must live as men. His humanity was united with divinity (2 Peter 1:3, 4). He lived without sinning through the same indwelling of the Holy Spirit we may experience. We need not retain even one sinful propensity.

That Power He Had Laid Aside

How did this emptying show itself in Jesus' daily life? On one occasion, the disciples were crossing the Sea of Galilee in a boat. Jesus was with them. A sharp tempest rose, threatening to sink the vessel. Jesus stood in the boat and prayed to His Father, "Shalom!" The sea was stilled.

When Jesus had been awakened to meet the storm, He was unafraid, in perfect peace. But He rested not in possession of almighty power.

It was not as "Master of earth and sea and sky" that He lay sleeping in the stern. That power

He had laid down. He said, "I can of Mine own self do nothing" (John 5:30). He trusted in the Father's might. It was in faith—trust in God's love and care—that Jesus rested, and the power of that word which stilled the storm was the power of God (Mark 4:35-41).

His By Right

He could have recovered His powers of deity at any time, for they were His by right (John 10:18; Philippians 2:6). But between the time of His entry into the human experience as a babe and the time of His crucifixion, He refused to employ powers He had laid aside. Why? Because we do not have such personal powers.

He wrought out a perfect example of how men and women may live with the same connection to our heavenly Father. He was subject to the same constraints in His flesh as we are in ours, for that flesh was, after all, the very same kind as ours (Hebrews 2:7-18). We may live in fallen flesh without joining ourselves to the deep and dangerous tendencies of that flesh. We may obey just exactly as He obeyed.

Conclusion

Still God, Jesus laid aside certain of His powers of divinity. This He did because He came to give the obedience, not of God to God, but of a man to God. This part of the *LGT* platform challenges us, showing us that we can live just as Jesus lived, because He lived just as we must live. He did not come as some kind of junior God or half-God to obey full God. He was fully God, very God, God undiminished, but He trusted in His Father for power just as we must today trust in Him for power.

If we cannot understand how Jesus lived, how will we know how to live as Christians? How will we have the unity that tells others that we know Christ? If we cannot know something of how far Jesus descended to meet us in our need, how will we know whether or not He can give us victory? He underwent an almost infinite humiliation for us in order to become as we are. Why? Because to have exercised His powers of deity while in our nature would have been self-defeating, and would have left us without His example.

The incarnation was spectacularly practical right here where we see Jesus as our Example. Our burning, irrevocable desire is to pursue and copy it, through the grace and strength He provides, all the way to the gates of heaven.

Discussion Questions

1. What is the incarnation?
2. According to Paul, what three things tend to be connected when error is presented on certain points?

3. Jesus became human, but did He choose to live under conditions identical to our own?

4. How was Jesus to obey, as God or as man?

5. While on earth, what powers were Jesus' by right?

6. While on earth, what powers did Jesus refuse to use?

7. Can we, like Christ, have an experience in which our thoughts offer Satan no foothold?

8. Did Jesus ever stop being God?

8. Jesus Tempted From Without and From Within

That which Jesus has not assumed He has not healed. He took our disordered humanity and was tempted both from without and within. Capable of choosing to sin, constantly He chose not to sin. In this sense, His entire earthly life was lived as we will live once we are sealed. Even after probation has closed, His power and presence continue with His followers. Today He grants them an experience of present and complete victory over sin.

Controversies Old and New

Back in the fourth century Gregory of Nazianzus uttered something quite profound. The occasion was the Apollinarian controversy. The center of this controversy was the theory of Apollinarius (a pastor, interestingly, in the city of Laodicea) that Jesus had a human body but a divine mind. This was not unlike saying that Jesus was like us from the neck down but not like us from the neck up.

In answer to this theory, Gregory countered, "If anyone has put his trust in Him [Jesus] as a man without a human mind, he is really bereft of mind and quite unworthy of salvation. For that which He [Jesus] has not assumed He has not healed; but that which is united with His Godhead is also saved. If only half Adam fell, then that which Christ assumes and saves may be half also; but if the whole of his nature fell, it must be united to the whole nature of Him that was begotten, and so be saved as a whole."

Gregory saw into the significance of the problem, not only of certain misguided teachers in his day, but in ours. The humanity of Christ is often presented as having been partly like Adam's and partly like ours. But since the Fall affected man in every aspect, we must have in Jesus a Savior who defeats sin in the same flesh as our own (Matthew 8:17). The humanity that He takes must be wholly affected by the Fall even as ours is, and the victory He wins over that disordered humanity must be just as complete.

Jesus Took Our Fallen Nature

Thus Jesus took our disordered humanity—not the nature of Adam before his Fall, but after. While Jesus was sinless (Hebrews 7:26), and never chose to sin (Hebrews 4:15), His humanity was the same disordered variety as our own. It had to be. Jesus had come to defeat sin in its own lair, on its home ground. Therefore He must meet sin in fallen human flesh. He must confront it in all of its strength. This we know is exactly what He did, for the Bible tells us:

For what the law could not do, in that it was weak through the flesh, God sending His own Son in the likeness [not "unlikeness"!] of sinful flesh, and for sin, condemned sin in the flesh: That the righteousness of the law might be fulfilled in us, who walk not after the flesh, but after the Spirit (Romans 8:3, 4).

In order to carry our sins He must walk in our flesh. If His stripes are going to heal us, then He must receive His stripes in our fallen kind of flesh (Isaiah 53:1-6). Jesus was a free agent, placed on probation at the risk of failure, as was Adam and as is man. Unless there is a possibility of yielding (Hebrews 2:18), temptation is no temptation. We resist temptation by faith laying firm hold upon divine power.

With every succeeding generation, the race has been further weakened. Like a photo-copied image itself photo-copied, and that image photo-copied from the copy, and the next photo-copied from that copy, each generation of the image is degraded compared to the one before. But what is true of our humanity since Adam fell was true also of Jesus' humanity. It was affected in exactly the same way. We are saddled with blurry, photocopy-copied humanity, and so was He. Yet He overcame (Revelation 3:21)!

Differences Between Jesus and Ourselves

There were some significant differences between Christ and us. He was God. We are not. As God, He had inherent rights to power as God. We do not. The value of His character is the character of the righteous God. Ours is not. We all have chosen to sin. He never did. Yet, the difference between His human equipment and our own?

None.

One other difference we shall here mention. Jesus, to successfully redeem man, must never sin. Just one sin on His part and the whole great controversy war would be lost. Satan would have proved his point. So Jesus lived out His time incarnate as human as we are, in the same flesh as our own, with the clamors and pulls of fallenness kept under, inch by inch, every step He walked, for 33 years (Matthew 26:39, 42; Mark 14:36; Luke 22:42; 1 Corinthians 9:27).

Our case is different. We all have sinned but we all have a Savior. Jesus volunteered to take our place that we might have a second trial, another testing, one more opportunity to choose God's righteous moral design for us. Jesus could not sin one time without losing all; we have sinned many times, yet, if we through His power forsake sin, we will be saved at last.

If Jesus' life is to have any meaning as an example for us, then it is crucial that He inherit just what we inherit. If our Lord took a perfect human nature, then He reconnected God and man's unfallen nature, but not God and fallen man. That gulf still needed to be bridged. But if Christ shared our fallen human nature, then He has bridged the whole gulf between God and fallen man. Then we have a Savior!

Life in the End-zone

Jesus lived His whole life beyond the end-zone, like the period at time's end during which probation for man will have closed (Revelation 22:11, 12). When probation closes, when redemption is finished and Jesus readies to return, the sanctuary in heaven will have ceased to operate as it always has before. Mediation for sin will have ceased. Willing believers will have stopped sinning through the power of the Holy Spirit. No new sins will ascend to be recorded in the sanctuary.

After probation closes, we are still empowered by Christ, who pledged never to leave us (Matthew 28:18-20), but during this fearful time, we will live, standing in the sight of a holy God without a Mediator. Our characters will have been purified from sin by the blood of Christ (Hebrews 9:14). Through the grace of God and a measure of strong effort on our part called faith (though not meritorious!), we will have become conquerors in the battle with evil.

Not only did Jesus live victoriously by the power of the Father just as we must, but He, like us, was tempted from the outside and from the inside (John 2:25; Hebrews 2:11, 14, 16-18; 4:15; Luke 22:42). His humanity pulled and clamored just as ours does. But He never chose to join Himself to those inclinations of His human organism. He never developed the habit patterns of sin, for He never sinned.

Conclusion

Jesus took our disordered human organism and consequently, was tempted both from without and from within. In order to heal our fallen humanity, He must accomplish His incarnation mission in our fallen humanity. He lived His entire life while on earth as we will live after we are sealed.

We all have sinned and come short of God's glory (Romans 3:23). We have cultivated habit patterns of sin—propensities to contend with, as well as inherited tendencies. Nevertheless, it gives us courage to face our own battles when we realize that Jesus fought the battle against inward inclination and kept His character pure.

In proving that a human being, encumbered with all the liabilities of human nature, could, by the power of the indwelling Spirit of God, obey His laws, freely and without coercion, Jesus showed that God's moral requirements are fair and that Satan has been lying. He showed us what He is willing to do for the last generation. His power, even after probation's close, will be available to us for victory over sin.

Discussion Questions

1. If Jesus did not in His incarnation take our humanity, then what could He not have done?

2. How did Jesus condemn sin?

3. Was Jesus' humanity the same kind as our own?

4. Whose life alone provides a pattern for how we will have to live after probation closes?

5. Was Jesus tempted both outwardly and inwardly?

6. To what inclinations did Jesus refuse to join Himself?

7. By obeying in a humanity encumbered by human liabilities and even our fallen nature, what does Jesus show us about God's requirements?

Atonement

Just as a correct understanding of how the Fall affected our human situation is vital, so is a correct understanding of the atonement. Is the atonement finished? No. It is in process and nears conclusion.

The cleansing of the sanctuary in heaven is connected to the cleansing of lives on earth. The atonement is not only external or merely theoretical. It is part of our own daily experience to bring us into full harmony with God. The atonement is not merely a "cashing in" of what Jesus earned at the cross, but includes our great High Priest sending the Holy Spirit to empower. The work done in us by the Holy Spirit is part of the atonement.

9. Jesus is Currently Making the Final Atonement

Jesus' atonement was promised in Eden. With His incarnation and then death as our Substitute upon the cross, His atoning work was begun. He rose from the dead and went to heaven in A.D. 31 to represent us before the Father, who received His sacrifice for us. Through that sacrifice we can be right with God as soon as we accept His gift of forgiveness and heart cleansing. In A.D. 1844 He entered the second apartment of the heavenly sanctuary, commencing the closing phase of His atonement. Today, Jesus is making the final atonement.

Atonement Promised in Eden

In the beginning, God had urged Adam and Eve to obey Him (Genesis 2:16, 17). Our race was given opportunity to bypass sin altogether. And yet, were they to be truly free, God could not force obedience. Satan bent his energies to the full when Eve came to the tree alone (Genesis 3:1-5). Very soon, but without a thought-through commitment to rebellion, Adam and Eve had chosen to disobey.

Before the great emergency, provision had been made. Jesus was "the Lamb slain from the foundation of the world" (Revelation 13:8). The Father and the Son did not ordain that sin should exist, but in giving created intelligences freedom, They foresaw its existence. They were prepared for the emergency when it developed. As soon as there was sin, there was a Savior.

Atonement was promised in Eden. In Genesis 3:15 God pledged that the Seed of the woman would triumph over the seed of the serpent. Jesus would come from the family line of Adam and Eve. He would open the way for man to be transformed from his disordered, rebel situation, to holiness and unselfishness. The divine image would be restored. God and man would walk together again (Genesis 3:8; Romans 8:29; Revelation 21:3)!

Identical in Kind

Why did Jesus descend from heaven to this planet? Why did He clothe Himself in our humanity? He took the same dramatically disordered human organism that we have because it was fallen man that needed salvation. If He would be sacrificed in our place, He must take the only kind of humanity truly identified with us.

A collie cannot run in a horse race. It might be the fastest-running collie dog on planet earth, but it is not a horse. Only horses can run in horse races. Jesus had to identify with our fallen human organism completely, in every way. This humanity must be unlike that of Adam before his fall, for Jesus came to die (Hebrews 2:14). Part of the incarnational purpose was to provide an offering, identical in kind, for those for whom the sacrifice was made.

In 4 B.C. Jesus came as a babe. Born into poverty, raised by Joseph and Mary, He grew to adulthood as do other children. He lived His life in the humanity that needs to be healed. And with His stripes we are healed (Isaiah 53:5; Matthew 8:17; 1 Peter 2:24). In A.D. 31 Jesus died on the cross in our place. The ladder of salvation was erected. At Calvary He hung between heaven and earth, linking God and man.

A perfect life was offered. A complete sacrificial atonement was presented. Sin had been defeated in fallen—not unfallen, or semi-fallen—humanity. Like had died for like, Kind for kind.

Christ as Victim, Christ as High Priest

Hanging on the tree, Jesus breathed His last, but the atonement still had to be mediated in some real way in heaven. Few Christians are aware that the sanctuary on earth was a representation of a heavenly pattern (Exodus 25:8, 9). Passages in Hebrews make clear the reality of the heavenly sanctuary:

> Now of the things which we have spoken this is the sum: We have such an High Priest, who is set on the right hand of the

throne of the Majesty in the heavens; A minister of the sanctuary, and of the true tabernacle, which the Lord pitched, and not man. For every high priest is ordained to offer gifts and sacrifices: wherefore it is of necessity that this man have somewhat also to offer. For if He were on earth, He should not be a priest, seeing that there are priests that offer gifts according to the law: Who serve unto the example and shadow of heavenly things, as Moses was admonished of God when he was about to make the tabernacle: for, See, saith He, that thou make all things according to the pattern showed to thee in the mount (Hebrews 8:1-5).

It was therefore necessary that the patterns of things in the heavens should be purified with these; but the heavenly things themselves with better sacrifices than these. For Christ is not entered into the holy places made with hands, which are the figures of the true; but into heaven itself, now to appear in the presence of God for us (Hebrews 9:23, 24).

While on earth He filled the role of sacrificial victim; now in heaven He fills the role of High Priest. While on earth He gave His life; now in heaven He as High Priest ministers the power of that life (Hebrews 7:16). While on earth He made provision for every man who would seek for salvation (Hebrews 2:9); from heaven He sends forth the helping strength of His Deity to make effectual in man the atonement being wrought out.

When can we be right with God? Need we wait until Jesus has finished His mediation in heaven? No! We can be right with Him just as soon as we accept His gift of heart cleansing (Isaiah 27:5; Romans 5:1). The downlink is functional today. The door stands open still.

For the Christian, heaven begins on earth. When we give our hearts to Him, He accepts us right where we are and forgives our sins. He takes us by the hand, He points us into the path where He is walking, and we set off together in the pathway of the Lamb slain for us. We have not at that moment arrived at our destination, but we are right with God and on the way. How wonderful it is to walk with Jesus!

Daily and Yearly Ministrations and 1844

Jesus at the time of His ascension to heaven in A.D. 31 commenced His work in the Holy Place. The system of ministry which God had instituted included the daily sacrifice and finished once a year with the Day of Atonement. Christ's work in heaven starting in A.D. 31 was equivalent to the earthly sanctuary's daily ministry.

The earthly services were but figures of the true. For 1,813 years after His resurrection, Jesus continued to serve as in the daily round of the earthly sacrifices, as our High Priest offering the grace of "mercy and ... help in time of need" (Hebrews 4:14, 16). He wished to share many more things with His people, but they could not yet bear them (John 16:12). With the passage of time, God's followers had veered off course, detouring into strong error. It would take centuries of reform to come back to where God could "cleanse the camp" of all sin (Leviticus 16:21, 22, 30).

The Yom Kippur, the Day of Atonement (Leviticus 16; 23:26-32), was a once a year symbol of God's ultimate plan to put away all sin from the universe forever (Daniel 8:14). It was a symbolic reminder, year after year, that at last, at the end, God would finish with the previews and accomplish the prefigured purpose.

In Daniel 8:14 He announced that the cleansing of the true sanctuary in heaven would begin in 2,300 days, meaning years (Numbers 14:34; Ezekiel 4:6). We know the starting point for that countdown, too: 457 B.C. (Daniel 9:25; Ezra 7:13). Twenty-three hundred years afterwards takes us to A.D. 1844. At that time Jesus moved from the Holy Place in heaven to the Most Holy.

In the yearly service the sins of the camp of Israel were cleansed. But in the present-day parallel at our end of time, from 1844 onward, the lives of men began at last to be evaluated. Person by person, each life professed to have been given to God is judged. Those who claim to believe in Him are His character witnesses. What is the testimony given through their lives? The watching universe sees and hears each story. With rapt attention they explore what actually happened in us when we connected with Jesus.

And so, the final atonement began in 1844. Presently it is under way; presently it is in process. In the sanctuary above Jesus is making the final atonement.

Conclusion

Jesus' incarnation and sacrificial death in our place on the cross were only the beginning of the atonement. His ministry in heaven since 1844 is necessary to complete the atonement.

Some voices today would like to de-emphasize the prophetic heritage of God's people. They would like to say that when Jesus died on the cross the atonement was then completed; that now, the Christian simply waits for Jesus to return. But the atonement was not finished at the cross. A perfect sacrifice was there offered, but for it to become effective for us, Christ's life must be manifest in ours. Jesus is now in the Most Holy Place of the heavenly sanctuary in process of completing the final atonement.

This is a practical point, truly pivotal, for it helps us to avoid the inevitably shrunken picture of the gospel that comes by limiting the atonement to the cross. Avoiding the Most Holy Place ministry of Christ in the heavenly sanctuary inevitably leads to avoiding most holy living while on earth. The *LGT* understanding of the atonement helps us see its meaning for our lives. It changes how we live today.

Discussion Questions

1. When did Jesus' heavenly sanctuary ministry begin?
2. What did Jesus begin to do in 1844?
3. As soon as there was sin, what else was there?
4. To make atonement, with whom must Jesus fully identify, and of the same kind fully be?
5. Why must His sacrifice of atonement be made in the same kind of humanity?
6. What does Jesus now send forth from heaven to us?
7. When can we have peace with God?
8. What did the yearly Yom Kippur service, in which the camp of Israel was cleansed of all sin, prefigure?

10. Cleansing in Heaven Connected to Cleansing on Earth

Neither Luther nor the Millerite Adventists living in 1844 finished the Reformation or understood the angel messages of Revelation 14 and 18. The cleansing of the heavenly sanctuary is connected to the cleansing and purifying of lives on earth. The sanctuary is cleansed when God has a people who have become so settled into the truth that they will never again be moved to doubt Him or to disobey known duty. The torrent of sin that has needed forgiveness is dried up. Christ's presence remains with those who have chosen Him. The Holy Spirit empowers obedience even after the ministry of forgiveness is closed.

The Reformation Left Unfinished

God, by His Holy Spirit, especially directs His servants on earth in the great movements that carry forward the work of salvation. Men are instruments in the hand of God. He employs them to accomplish His purposes of grace. Each has his part to act and to each is granted a measure of light, adapted to the necessities of his time. We are given enough light to perform the work which God has given us to do.

Even so, no man, however honored of Heaven, has ever attained to a full understanding of the great plan of redemption. The divine purpose in the work for his own time is never fully known by finite man. Neither the most sincere preacher nor Spirit-led Reformer has yet understood all.

The Reformation is left unfinished. Not even Seventh-day Adventists have finished the work of God. We have been slow to grasp "present truth," but the messages of Daniel and Revelation are now coming to fruition. At last we are learning our place in Bible history. Mighty truths are unfolding before our very eyes.

God has set His people on the pathway to an entirely different religious experience. He wants us to complete the Reformation. There will be a final generation. One day the gospel light shines undiminished as it did in the first century under apostolic preaching. The people who permit that light to fill them will be used of God to end evil once and for all. This is the purpose of the gospel!

The River of Sin Dried Up

One of the most urgent messages of the sanctuary doctrine since 1844 is that something special is required of God's followers in terms of character development that may not have been as crucial to the development of the church until now. To Adventists it was given to grasp the reality of Christ's ministry in the heavenly sanctuary and of the Investigative Judgment presently under way. The cleansing of the heavenly sanctuary is connected to the cleansing and purifying of lives on earth.

Our God urges us to "sin not," and "Go and sin no more" (Exodus 20:20; Psalm 4:4; John 5:14; 8:11; 1 Corinthians 15:34; 1 John 2:1), to purify ourselves even as Jesus is pure (1 John 3:3), to walk even as Jesus walked (1 John 2:6). The only way we will do that is by living righteous lives— lives in which unreserved obedience to Him is manifest. When we are so settled into the truth, both doctrinally and experientially, that we cannot be moved, we will no longer sin. We will stop sending sins into the heavenly sanctuary to be forgiven.

Our connection with Him will be so firm that we will never again be moved to doubt His goodness, His wisdom, or His rightness. We will recognize that His requirements are for our protection. We will trust His instructions, for at last we will know His voice (John 10:1-6). All this Satan has denied and misrepresented, but today he is being proven wrong.

Throughout our lives we have sent forth a river of sin, washing up to the heavenly sanctuary, there to be purified. Each and every one of those sins has to be removed by Christ. But the day approaches when the torrent of sin will be dried up; when known duties will be fulfilled; when we will be living by every word that proceeds from God's mouth (Deuteronomy 8:3). The fullness of His Spirit will be manifest.

God is so good and we, His people, will become so resolute in doing His goodness, that we will stop sinning. We live in the Spirit and cease to fulfill the lust of the flesh (Galatians 5:16).

Full light will be shining upon our paths, and full cooperation will be evident in our lives. God will have healed us from all our iniquities. Satan will not be able to claim that Jesus has not completely saved His people from their sins (Matthew 1:21; Zechariah 3:1-5).

Jesus has purified them by the special outpouring of the Holy Spirit (Acts 3:19), and there is no longer any need to forgive sin in His people, even ignorant sin, because no more sin will be there. His people can live in the sight of a holy God, because of His imparted righteousness, without any blemish of sin whatsoever contaminating their thoughts or actions.

A Special Work of Purification

Now, while the Investigative Judgment is going forward in heaven, while the sins of believers are being removed from the sanctuary in heaven, there is a special work of purification, of putting away of sin, among God's people on earth. When this work shall have been accomplished, the followers of Christ will be ready for His appearing. Then the church which our Lord at His coming is to receive to Himself will be a "glorious church, not having spot, or wrinkle, or any such thing" (Ephesians 5:27).

We now are living in this joyful and solemn time. Our self-inflicted scars seem innumerable. Our sins have been legion. But so are our opportunities! It is the privilege of each one so to live that God will approve and bless him. It is not the will of our heavenly Father that we should ever be under condemnation and darkness. We may go to Jesus and be cleansed, and stand before the law without shame or remorse. Praise Him for the opportunity of being made like our Lord here and now!

The cross of Calvary challenges, and will finally vanquish every earthly and hellish power. It is the great center of attraction; for on it Christ gave up His life for the human race. This sacrifice was offered for the purpose of restoring man to his original perfection. It was offered to give him an entire transformation of character, and make him at last more than a conqueror. The cross stands before the doorway into the sanctuary.

Now, while our great High Priest is making the atonement for us, we should seek to become present overcomers through Christ. Not even by a thought could our Savior be brought to yield to the power of temptation. Satan finds in human hearts some point where he can gain a foothold, some sinful desire cherished, by means of which his temptations assert their power.

But consider Jesus. He said, "The prince of this world cometh, and hath nothing in Me" (John 14:30). Satan could find nothing in Christ that would enable him to gain the victory. Jesus had kept His Father's commandments, and there was no sin in Him that Satan could use to his advantage. This is the condition in which those must be found who shall stand victoriously (Revelation 3:21).

Help After the Close of Probation

Even after the sanctuary is closed, we will have the help of the Holy Spirit (Matthew 28:18-20). No, not for forgiveness of continual sinning; that ministry will have closed. God's people will have ceased from sin. But in order to live godly lives, we will still need His power. We will always need it, and it will not be withdrawn in the last generation.

Conclusion

Reformation has become more slogan than reality; deformation has slowed the progress of God's people. Protest against error has slipped from generation to generation. Too many descendants of the Reformers have settled into accommodating untruth. But God will have His finished work. Although company after company from the Lord's army may join the foe, tribe after tribe from the ranks of the enemy will break free to unite with the commandment-keeping people of God.

The cleansing underway in the heavenly sanctuary today reflects the cleansing in the lives of Jesus' followers on earth today. The High Priest is mediating, the Intercessor is interceding, the Carpenter is crafting character, the earth is being lightened with His glory. Practical? For the *LGT* Christian, we want to know where to find our Savior and how to let Him do His work as our High Priest. We want to mount up ever higher. God is not yet vindicated in His people.

As followers of Christ, our lives offer evidence as to whether God or Satan has been right in the great controversy. We need to be reminded that the battle between good and evil did not end at the cross, but is being played-out in our hearts and minds today.

Discussion Questions

1. Has any Reformer ever had a perfect understanding of God's purposes?
2. Is the Protestant Reformation finished?
3. What movement is called of God to bring the Reformation to completion?

4. How does the cleansing of the heavenly sanctuary involve us today?

5. Why was Christ's sacrifice offered?

6. Now, while our great High Priest is making the atonement for us, for what should we seek?

7. After the close of probation, will we still have the presence of the Holy Spirit?

Delay and Hastening

God will not close probation for the world until (1) a significant portion of His remnant vindicates His government, proving that His way of life can be lived on earth and showing Satan wrong; and (2), His willing followers proclaim a credible witness to all nations. To believe that Jesus is in a holding pattern is one of the most sobering concepts that anyone on earth can encounter. Our task is to remove the conditions that keep Jesus waiting.

The delay and hastening themes in Scripture show that God has locked His theology to His goal. If the Church has yet to arrive at the goal, then she has yet to be the gospel's fully faithful witness (Matthew 24:14). God has already decided to give us the kingdom; He has already designed righteousness by faith to do this. We must surrender our strange fascination with popular Christendom and hear His simple, profound description of those who have found righteousness by faith. Why do we delay?

11. Delaying the Second Coming Through a Half-Gospel

Jesus' Second Coming could have occurred within the generation that proclaimed the 1844 messages, but the same sins that kept ancient Israel out of the promised land have delayed the entrance of modern Israel into the heavenly Canaan. Unbelief, worldliness, unconsecration, and strife among the Lord's professed people have kept us in this world of sin and sorrow so many years.

Postponement and Delay

The Second Coming could not occur on planet earth until after the final atonement was made—until after the sanctuary began to be cleansed—until after A.D. 1844. When it comes to the ultimate cleansing of the sanctuary God is waiting for the last stragglers (Revelation 7:1-3; Genesis 33:13, 14). But this is not the only biblical record of postponement of His purposes. Another primary record of postponement was the 40-year delay between the Hebrews' leaving bondage in Egypt (Exodus 13:3) and their entrance at last into Canaan (Numbers 13; 14). This delay was not God's preferred will (Hebrews 3:16-19). But when the people insisted on deciding otherwise than God had already decided, He permitted them to experience the consequences they had thus chosen (Deuteronomy 1:22-40). He could not work through them as He had planned.

Jesus told His disciples that He had many things to say to them that they could not then hear (John 16:12). He said that He would, while away, be preparing a place for them in His Father's house (John 14:1-3). His work is the cleansing of the heavenly sanctuary. The round of ceremonies linked with the earthly sanctuary were representations of the pardon and power that will be fully manifested in God's people at time's end (Daniel 8:13, 14; Hebrews 8:1-5; 9:23, 24; Leviticus 16).

The cleansing of the typical sanctuary on earth was a once a year event. With a cleansed camp the cycle of sin was closed (Leviticus 16:22). In the final generation comes at last the antitypical parallel. It points to the Second Coming. In both cases, the focus is on sin removal and the deliverance of a group who have cooperated with God.

The Church Now Lives in a Circular Pattern

Delay means that the church now lives in a circular pattern, doing needless laps in the desert, rolling up useless miles on the odometer. It means death in the wilderness for one or more generations. It means the scorching heat of the Negev rather than the cool mountain streams of Canaan.

When the Hebrews came to the edge of Canaan and then failed, they were auditioning for the role of Laodicea. They were laying down the pattern. Thinking they were rich and increased with goods and in need of nothing (Revelation 3:17), they actually left out of their reckoning the God who had delivered them. Then they reversed direction completely and decided that they could not conquer Canaan— the land that God had promised (Exodus 3:8, 17; 23:20, 23, 28-33; 33:1, 2; 34:11, 24). Already they had heard God's decision to give it to them. But they manifested unbelief, worldliness, unconsecration, and strife.

Unbelief, by refusing to have faith. Hebrews 3:19 and 4:2 show that they would not trust in God their Father who had led them across the desert. They preferred to wallow in discussion of all the real and imagined failings of human leadership. Although He had already determined they would enter the promised land, they left Him out of their planning; they chose to operate by sight and not by faith (2 Corinthians 5:17). They decided the invasion of Canaan was hopeless.

Worldliness, by thinking of the leeks and the onions and the fleshpots of Egypt (Numbers 11:4-6). The restaurants on the road to hell have such flavorful food. Yes, in Egypt they had been in bondage of slavery, but there had been food in abundance: fish, onions, and melons. They forgot their bondage but remembered the food. They despised the diet God had prepared, loathing His manna.

Unconsecration, by refusal to be committed to His vision for them (Proverbs 29:18; 2 Chronicles 20:20). He wanted to heal them, He wanted to grow them, strengthen them, to help them have the self-discipline that as slaves they had never developed. It was one thing to obey under duress, under the whip and the scourge, under coercion—but something else to do willingly what was asked of one from an appreciation of the character of the one asking.

Strife, by failure to recognize and consent to God's leading. There was strife among the Lord's professed people. While the commands of God for their benefit were ignored, the people planned for themselves. Although God had been explicit about His plans for them, they were prepared to elect new officers and return into Egypt (Numbers 14:1-4). God's loyalists sought to stem the enveloping tide of emotion and apostasy, but the rebels would not hear. The people prepared to assassinate them (Numbers 14:10). Rebels always end up destroying themselves or each other.

Have We Delayed the Second Coming of Christ?

But how have we delayed the coming of Christ? Is that even possible? Consider:

1. The Hebrew sanctuary system was a yearly round of teaching events with a final cleansing of the camp at year's end. The issue? Sin removal. End result? People and camp were cleansed. Daniel 8:13, 14 foretells that the actual heavenly sanctuary will be cleansed just prior to Christ's return. The parallel for our day, therefore, is the removal of sin from God's people.

2. The journey from Egypt to Canaan that should have taken only weeks was, on account of the people's own lack of faith, turned into a 40-year wilderness death-march. The people, who refused to enter in after God had saved them from Egypt and preserved them through the desert journey, closed-out their parched lives in the desert still. But their children entered in. The people delayed the accomplishment of the divine purpose. The unfaithful were removed in the wilderness. The true followers, Caleb and Joshua, were able to go in after the delay.

3. After the Jews had rejected Christ, the Greek Scriptures written following the death of Jesus testified abundantly of the blessed hope, His Second Coming. The Greek Scriptures, as well as the Hebrew (Daniel 9:25), told of His purpose to remove sin from His people (Matthew 1:21). They testified of a time when probation for sin and sinners

would close (Revelation 22:11, 12) and Jesus would return "without sin unto salvation" (Hebrews 9:28); and that the redeemed would be changed, made "without fault and blameless before His throne" (Revelation 14:5).

4. The gospel has yet to truly produce a people without spot and blameless, without wrinkle or any such thing (Ephesians 5:27-29). Jesus has not appeared because His people have not yet fully readied themselves. The wedding is delayed. Christ still waits, standing at the altar (Revelation 19:7, 8).

5. Some 2,000 years have elapsed since Christ's first coming. That is a very long time—longer than between the worldwide flood and Moses; longer than between the Exodus and the time of Christ; longer than the existence of Israel as a kingdom; almost 2,000 years since Christ's sacrificial death for us on the cross—which event supposedly, according to popular theology, resolved everything.

The above lines of thought help us to understand how there can be a delay in God's purposes. The sanctuary service showed that God had intervened, introducing a system whereby sin removal would be accomplished. Daniel shows that this was a shadow predicting an end-time cleansing of God's people. The wilderness wandering of the Hebrews shows that God's people delayed the fulfillment of His purposes for them because of their unfaithfulness. The promise of the Second Coming and the Scriptural insistence on sin removal echoes the work of the earthly sanctuary. All will acknowledge that God has not yet produced an overcoming people. Finally, the fact that at least 2,000 years will separate His First coming from His Second, suggests that the divine purpose remains unaccomplished.

The Scriptures include several incidents of postponement that we have not explored, including the delay of the destruction of Sodom while Lot fled to Zoar (Genesis 19:18-25), the parable of the delayed Bridegroom (Matthew 25:1-13), the parable of the unfaithful servant (Luke 12:35-48), the delay of the sealing angels on account of the unpreparedness of God's people (Revelation 7:1-3), and more. Nevertheless, the Bible establishes a history of delays and postponements in the footsteps of God's people.

Conclusion

One of the primary biblical records of postponement is the delay of Israel in entering Canaan. This history is unambiguous. More closely than we would like to admit, we have been repeating the history of that people, and too often, repeating the very mistakes made by them so long ago.

Christ could have arrived in His Second Coming glory shortly after 1844. But the implications of Bible history mostly have been left strangely unaddressed. Headstone engravers still ply their trade on planet earth. But the cemeteries are getting full. The earth travails under the transgression of its inhabitants waiting for the sons and daughters of God to be revealed (Romans 8:18-22).

God voluntarily limits Himself. If He did not, no flesh would be saved. He waits for the last generation because He is making a point. And He hasn't made it. Yet. Our generation can and should be the one to show what happens when man cooperates fully with God. But we must break out of our own cycle of sinning that delays His purposes. Recognition that we have had to remain here in this world because of our insubordination is important, for it is only as we realize we have gone round another lap that we begin watching for the off-ramp that finally can take us home.

Discussion Questions

1. What is one of the primary biblical records of postponement?

2. Christ could have come shortly after what year?

3. How does the Hebrews' delay in entering Canaan parallel the situation at the end of time?

4. In what kind of a pattern does the church now live?

5. What are four particular sins that kept the Hebrews from entering the promised land? Have God's people today been guilty of the same? Have we taken any specific steps to resolve these issues?

6. What is the sanctuary system all about?

7. God is making a point. What is it?

12. Hastening the Second Coming and Embracing the Harvest Principle

Heaven has put it in our power by conse-crated, Christ-reflecting lives to hasten Jesus' return. God will wait for the maturing of Christian character in a significant number of people as the chief condition determining those events, such as the latter rain, loud cry, sealing, and Sunday law, which affect the time when probation for the world shall close, and thus the time of the Second Coming.

Holy Lives Hasten Christ's Return

If it is possible for us to delay the Second Coming, then logically, we may, through cooperation with God, be able to hasten or contribute to a more rapid occurrence of the same event. Has God placed this glorious possibility within reach?

The Scriptures provide our answer. Second Peter 3:11, 12: "Seeing then that all these things shall be dissolved, what manner of persons ought ye to be in all holy conversation and godliness, looking for and hasting unto the coming of the day of God, wherein the heavens being on fire shall be dissolved, and the elements shall melt with fervent heat?"

In light of the imminent judgment of the earth, the impending destruction of the world as we know it, we are called to give an unambiguous witness. Our life testifies. "What manner of persons ought ye to be in all holy conversation and godliness?" The power of this extraordinary witness is seen in the phrase "looking for and hasting," or "hoping for and causing to occur faster," or "hastening" (marginal reading). Hastening means to cause something to happen sooner than it otherwise would. The Bible does not include this idea at random. The Holy Spirit wants us to grasp the extraordinary power of holy living.

Lines of Evidence

At least five lines of thought help us see the possibility of hastening. First, as we have already observed, 2 Peter 3:11, 12 urges us, in light of the speedily approaching end, to live in such a manner that the coming of Christ is accelerated.

Second, remember the ancient events involving Job. He was a faithful man, and when Satan came to dispute with God, it was God who brought forth Job's name. God presented Job as an example of one who from pure motives faithfully served Him. Job's life of faith hastened the day of his testing. He was tested specifically because it was safe to trust him. He could be a character witness for God because he was a willing believer and a close friend. God knew it. God permitted the test. Through Job's trials evidence for the vindication of God's goodness was given.

Third, Revelation 12 shows that the end-time conflict is between Satan and the remnant church. In Romans 16:20 Paul reminds us that Christ will crush Satan under our feet. The promise of Genesis 3:15 is realized, not alone through Jesus' life and death, but through the holy lives and death to self manifest in His people in the end-time. Luke 10:19 shows that when Christ sent out the 70, He gave them authority to tread on all the strength of Satan. Those who herald Christ's return, in following their Lord, will tread upon the serpent and bring tidings of final peace (Isaiah 52:7, 8).

Fourth, Revelation 14:12 shows that at time's end God points to the people matured by His gospel. "Here are they," He says. The sooner their characters are developed, the sooner the adversary will be defeated. The sooner the gospel harvest is ripe, the sooner our Lord reaps His harvest of trustworthy, willing believers.

Fifth, the 490 and 2,300 day/year prophecies also help. God gave first to the Hebrews the opportunity of ushering in everlasting righteousness. From the starting point of 457 B.C., 490 years were granted (Daniel 9:24-27; Numbers 14:34; Ezekiel 4:6). Had the people then been faithful, they would have ushered in everlasting righteousness—hastened it—by some 1,810 years. But they did not. So probation for that people as a nation closed in A.D. 34, and the gospel was entrusted to the Gentiles. When the Jews failed, the time allotted for them was ended (Daniel 9:24, "determined," literally, "cut off"). The Jews could, by being faithful, have hastened the arrival of righteousness.

To hasten is to cooperate with heaven's purposes completely. Only this can open the way for His working out of the gospel's purpose (Romans 8:29; Ephesians 5:25-27).

The Harvest Principle

One of the most crucial concepts for God's people today is to understand what has been called the Harvest Principle. We present it in four simple points:

1. God made man in His image and likeness (Genesis 1:26, 27). On the basis of this noble heritage of inwrought value, relentlessly and irrevocably, He chooses to honor the freedom He gave when He made us in His image. He will not coerce us to live His way. He refuses to treat us as robots, choosing the longer route of freedom (Joshua 24:15; Romans 6:16). He permits the delays that arise because of our less than full commitment to His truth. At the same time He insists upon the hastening that our full commitment would bring.

The road from Eden to Eden passes directly through the twin cities of free choice and divine respect. God never takes the bypass. His commitment to these principles is part of His character. He is the Lord and He changes not (Malachi 3:6).

2. The plan of salvation has a goal. God is like the farmer (Mark 4:26-29). The farmer plants his crops with a goal in mind. He labors with the eventual harvest ever in sight. He toils not in vain but with an eye to the fruit that is growing. While Jesus hung on the cross in the giving of His life for us, one thought only brought comfort: the desire that the Father would see the travail of His soul, and be satisfied (Isaiah 53:11). That by the death-tasting experience Jesus passed through for us (Hebrews 2:9), the righteous Servant would make many righteous servants (Malachi 3:1-4).

He would bear their iniquities (Isaiah 53:11). He would empower their lives. He would, in His people, find 144,000 credible character witnesses (Revelation 14:1-5). Mature character would show in its richness the power of God unto salvation (Romans 1:16). The universe was not subjected to the horror of sin to no purpose (Romans 8:18-22). Heaven has a non-negotiable goal: the manifestation of the sons and daughters of God, men and women who can be entrusted with eternal life.

3. The approximate time of harvest is known, but the farmer keeps his eye on the maturation of fruit to see exactly when the crop is ripe and ready. "So is the kingdom of God, as if a man should cast seed into the ground; and should sleep, and rise night and day, and the seed should spring and grow up, he knoweth not how. For the earth bringeth forth fruit of herself; first the blade, then the ear, after that the full corn in the ear. But when the fruit is brought forth, immediately he putteth in the sickle, because the harvest is come" (Mark 4:26-29).

First, the stalk; the sprouting blade cuts through surface, rising above the soil. After a period of growth, next the kernel of wheat appears on the stalk. At last, when the crop reaches maturity, the full kernel in the head of wheat appears. Yet, all this is only prelude; the climax of the cycle comes when the farmer puts in the sickle. Matured wheat is harvested. This is the goal. Farmers don't plant seed because they enjoy weeding; they plant seed in expectation of a harvest worthy of their efforts.

4. Jesus must wait until the gospel seed has produced a sizable group of Christians in the last generation. The harvest should have ripened decades ago (Revelation 7:1-3; 14:1-5).

Jesus offers the help we need to become His special representatives of grace, power, and love, so that we can do our part to turn our generation into the last on earth. "And I looked, and behold a white cloud, and upon the cloud one sat like unto the Son of Man, having on His head a golden crown, and in His hand a sharp sickle. And another angel came out of the temple, crying with a loud voice to Him that sat on the cloud, Thrust in Thy sickle, and reap: for the time is come for Thee to reap; for the harvest of the earth is ripe. And He that sat on the cloud thrust in His sickle on the earth; and the earth was reaped" (Revelation 14:14-16).

The close of probation is not an arbitrary moment. Everything is ready to go as soon as the harvest is ripe! Is God less God because He permits man's actions to hasten or delay Christ's Second Advent? No. If man cooperates fully with God, God can carry forward His purposes on schedule. If man cooperates reluctantly, half-heartedly, or only partially, God will delay His plans. Like the farmer, He waits for the maturity of gospel seed in the lives of men and women. He calls us to cooperate with Him in hastening this world's harvest of mature followers who are a credit to the seed He planted.

Christ is Waiting

The difference in the final generation is that at last God's expectation will be clearly understood in one generation by a significant number. At last there will be a people who not only see what God is waiting for but will allow Him to fulfill His plan in them. Under the full blaze of gospel glory they give to God all the room He needs to make them new.

This final generation cooperates more fully with God's purposes than any previous generation. They are the end result of His 6,000-year garden patch. Six millennia of light shining down from heaven is at last reflected in men and women who have reached the gospel's purpose—the maturity of the stature of Christ (Ephesians 4:13). The light of changed lives shines heavenward at earth's midnight, a time when champions have been few.

Christ is waiting with longing desire for the manifestation of Himself in His church. When the character of Christ shall be perfectly reproduced in His people, then He will come to claim them as His own. It is the privilege of every Christian not only to look for but to hasten the coming of our Lord Jesus Christ. When we receive His cleansing, He will walk with us through the closing. How quickly then the whole world will be sown with the seed of the gospel, the last great harvest ripened, and Christ come to gather the precious grain.

Our Most Urgent Task

The most urgent task facing us is to hasten the Advent, to do in this generation what could have and should have been done by every generation since 1844. We need to remember our unique purpose. A group's sense of mission is always but one generation away from oblivion. It takes only one generation for any organization to lose its identity. The torch of truth is heavy in sleepy hands, and sinks imperceptibly to the ground in absence of utmost vigilance.

We must live under a sense of mission and relate everything in our lives to it. Many want Jesus' power without His character, but there is no changing the principles by which Heaven works. We will not find a person with His character without His power, any more than we would find the flame without the heat.

Many last-day events are held in suspension until this "cleansing" reaches that point where God will not be embarrassed to give His end-time people the promised latter rain (Deuteronomy 11:14; Jeremiah 3:3; Joel 2:23, 24; Zechariah 10:1; James 5:7). The eyes of the unfallen universe are not on this world's dreary parade of wars, famines, and natural disasters as they try to figure out when Jesus will return. Neither should ours be. God's people should not be spectators watching the parade of world events; actually, their journey is the parade for which all the universe has been waiting. Heavenly beings have been anxiously longing for God's professed people to cooperate with Him in hastening the Advent (2 Peter 3:12).

Conclusion

In *LGT*, we acknowledge not only that God's people have delayed the Second Coming, but that Heaven has put it in our power to hasten it. The Bible tells us that holy living at time's end has an impact on the great controversy war.

The story of Job is the great controversy in miniature. When God brought up the topic of His friend Job, Satan pressed his claim that even Job served God from selfish motives. This was yet another Luciferian untruth, and God challenged his faulty claims. In the end, Job's life gave evidence in favor of the goodness of God and the rightness of His ways.

Back in Genesis the promise was given of a Messiah coming to crush Satan fatally under His feet. But today, long after the cross, Jesus still lives, and so does Satan. The same Bible tells us that Jesus did not at the cross complete the process of crushing our foe. Paul looked forward to the time, in the last generation, when Jesus will finish flattening the great accuser under the very feet of the accused (Romans 16:20). Holy lives count in the great controversy war!

The Bible contains the Harvest Principle, the teaching that by manifesting the deepest consecration to Christ, our lives can speed the time of final harvest when Jesus shall come.

We search, with Holy Spirit-illumined audacity, for the openings our Father gives to those who are entirely on His side. Fully committed men and women will feel the heat of the fire in the furnace (Daniel 3) because they are at the front edge of God's will, a soldiery armed, a movement primed for the struggle ahead. Their confidence is in their General Jesus. At His command they are marching to Zion.

Discussion Questions

1. Why was Job tested?
2. Whose feet are involved in crushing Satan?
3. Does God depend on human beings in determining when Jesus will return?
4. What word best describes the kind of witness God would like to give to the world today?
5. Can you describe all four elements of the Harvest Principle?
6. Can we, by our lives, cause the Second Coming to occur sooner than it otherwise would?
7. For what does God wait as the chief condition determining when probation for the world shall close, and Christ's return occur?

Great Controversy and Decision Time

One day good will triumph over evil finally and irrevocably. It will be the grand finale. If the waiting seems unduly long, realize that the reward will be beyond measure. The universe will be rendered eternally secure. The last generation will explain and show what God can do when He has fully committed people.

We love God. We love what He is like. We agree with His government. We seek it. Converts to Jesus are not attracted by harsh people, but friendly; they are the ones who most resemble God. Our goal therefore is to best resemble Him in character and so attract others to His kingdom.

13. Character Witnesses to the Great Healer

More than forensic declarations only, the gospel is primarily concerned with telling the truth about God as our Best Friend. He is more concerned with our healing than with legal pronouncements. In the great controversy, His character witnesses tell the story of their deliverance.

The Reformation Hindered

The Dark Ages existed as a very deep hole. The Reformers did not leap onto the scene in one bound. Error was very strong; the darkness, apart from divine intervention, impenetrable. Even with Wycliffe, Hus, Luther, and the long list of Reformers following after, recovery was only an incremental, step by step process.

The deep error of Roman Catholicism was a turn from the wholistic Hebrew concepts about man and his restoration, to a narrow, legal, church/state mysticism. As this apostasy matured, it came to be understood that man was saved by his works, and those works, in order to sanctify, must be sanctioned by the Church. Against that background of error, the Reformers bent their best energies toward reform.

But the strongest humans are frail, and especially so with reference to ingrained patterns of thinking. Those enfolded in long-established cultural expectation are often unaware of their blinders. Ingrained in the minds of the Reformers Luther and Calvin was the philosophy of predestination.

According to this teaching, God predestinates some to salvation and some to destruction. Some, by the moving of the divine will, are chosen to be righteous, while others are fated to be evil. One group is cast as heroes, the other, villains. There are no real choices or risks in the conflict between good and evil. Human free will makes no significant contribution in human destiny.

Is this good news? Salvation becomes pre-salvation. Saving others becomes reciting the script already written in heaven. Puppet-strings are attached to human minds, mouths, and hearts. Nothing is proven to the universe; the only principle presented about God is that no one in heaven or on earth can override His sovereignty.

The truth? God's character is at the center of the great controversy. Yes, God is more powerful than Satan. But He permitted Satan time to demonstrate his evil principles. God's character and His government are morally right. Satan's are morally wrong. The entire universe is watching the consequences of God's principles and Satan's. God refuses to override the choices made by men and women as they decide whom they want to trust.

God's Character is the Center

If we see God as a glowering gatekeeper or a frowning judge standing ready to throw thunderbolts when we don't live up to His expectations, then we will be less likely to appreciate Him and trust Him for His character. But He does not want the service of fear, from angels or from man (2 Timothy 1:7; 1 John 4:18). He does not force the will of any (Joshua 24:15).

What He actually desires is that the creatures of His hands shall love Him because He is worthy of love and trust. He wants us to obey because we have an intelligent appreciation of His wisdom, justice, and goodness. Do we respect these qualities? Then we will be drawn toward Him in admiration (Romans 2:4). Our homage must spring from love for His character.

Jesus does not wish to be known by us as the great prosecutor but as the Great Physician. One who heals is easier to love than one who condemns. He has no intention of papering-over our sins with finely wrought legal arguments. He wants to cure us of sin.

Can Jesus Really Heal Us?

Someone has been hurt. He arrives at the hospital and after emergency treatment begins his recovery. His condition slowly improves. Over the course of his stay at the hospital, forms are signed dealing with insurance, treatment, and medication. A trail of paperwork began when he was admitted. Everything pertaining to his stay at the hospital, and medical treatment received, is carefully recorded.

The paperwork without the treatment would be a lie; the recovery without the paperwork would be ill-documented. A good hospital will have both, and physicians and patients will be able to mark the healing process. Thus it will become clear whether anyone is really being made well or not. Can the doctors heal? This is the same question the universe asks of Jesus: can He really heal? Is our Doctor Jesus a glorified charlatan who can't produce what He promises, or One who has given His utmost to make man holy? His character is the crux of the great controversy and this is the question that needs answering!

A similar question was asked by the leper. "And, behold, there came a leper and worshipped Him, saying, Lord, if Thou wilt, Thou canst make me clean. And Jesus put forth His hand, and touched him, saying, I will; be thou clean. And immediately his leprosy was cleansed. And Jesus saith unto him, See thou tell no man; but go thy way, show thyself to the priest, and offer the gift that Moses commanded, for a testimony unto them" (Matthew 8:2-4).

The leper needed no convincing of Jesus' authority; his question was, "Jesus, do you care enough for a miserable leper to heal me? What is your character like? Do you value me? Am I included in the war between good and evil, or am I just a spectator? A write-off?"

What then is our testimony? Does our experience testify to a placebo-giving fake, or an effective, sympathizing Physician who truly heals (Hebrews 2:17, 18)? Do the Father, Son, and Holy Spirit care? As participants in the great controversy war, our lives testify one way or the other as to what They do for us, and what we truly think of Them (Revelation 12:11).

Who is Safe to Save?

The universe is watching. The universe will see the consequences of rebellion in final display, ending with the horror of the seven last plagues (Revelation 15:1-4). Who is safe to save? What kind of earth rebels does God propose to trust with eternal life? Will our Lord's judgment receive hearty endorsement at last?

God already knows what we are individually. But He wants others to see the evidence, to make up their own minds as to whether Jesus is fair when He makes up His kingdom. The Investigative Judgment since 1844 is a matter of making more faithful bridesmaids (Matthew 25:1-13) and separating sheep from goats (Matthew 25:31-46)—

in other words, cleansing human temples from the defilement of sin.

Jesus is Our Intercessor

Christ is in the heavenly sanctuary as our High Priest (Hebrews 4:14-16). And what is He doing? Making atonement for us, cleansing the sanctuary from the sins of His people. Then we must by faith enter the sanctuary with Him; the work must be begun in the sanctuary of our souls. We are to cleanse ourselves from all defilement (Ezekiel 37:23; Ephesians 5:26; 1 John 1:7, 9). We must "cleanse ourselves from all filthiness of the flesh and spirit, perfecting holiness in the fear of God" (2 Corinthians 7:1).

If I should see a man with a baseball bat entering the room behind your back, my instincts would be to intercede and do all I could to keep him from hurting you. I would be your "intercessor" at that point in your life, standing between you and the evil one. Jesus is doing just that every hour of the day and night for you through His angels and the Holy Spirit (1 Timothy 2:5; Hebrews 8:6; 9:5). We can count on His powerful intercessions in our lives today, even as we have been counting on the fact that He died for us on that horrible cross!

The Best Friend we ever had—Jesus—died on that cross (Proverbs 18:24). For us. He is Creator and Judge. He is Deity, yes. But He is also

Healer, Elder Brother, Spouse, and Best Friend. How would you feel if your best human friend died to save you? Think about that for awhile. Then realize—Jesus is your best human friend. And He lives today as your High Priest, doing for you what the Holy Spirit did for Him— helping you to be an overcomer—giving real grace to help in time of need (Titus 2:11-14; Hebrews 4:16).

What is the natural result of all this? Simple. We want to tell others of His goodness. We want our character to testify to the goodness of His character. The questions of who will be saved and of whether or not God's character will at last be vindicated, are two completely separate topics. Continual character surrender is what it takes to be saved; full character maturity is what it takes to vindicate God's character.

Perfection does not save man, but it does contribute to the vindication of God's character. Whether or not I am saved is a much less important question than whether or not God is found to be just when He is judged (Romans 3:4; Revelation 14:6, 7). Not upon the former, but upon the latter question hinges the ultimate security of God's government and fulfillment at last of the promised Second Coming. By telling the truth about God to the world, we vote for His character. And the polls are ready to close.

Conclusion

The Reformation isn't over. The last generation has a commission to finish it. God wants us to love Him on the basis of a true understanding of Him. Entwining error about the character of God prevents that; thus every error that misrepresents God must be uprooted (Matthew 15:13). The biblical picture of God is much more that of a Healer than that of a grim judge.

But where is the evidence? Where is the final argument so that God can say to Satan, "You have not proved your allegations; case dismissed"? Our Father in heaven does not propose merely to assert that He is right, but, through those who believe in Him, actually to demonstrate His goodness. We have a part in the great controversy war.

One day soon, as we continue to abide in Christ, walking into the light He daily gives, making a habit of not saying "No" to known duty, we will be part of that great host that declares God's judgments to be "true and righteous" (Revelation 19:2). We will be part of the eternal answer to Satan's lies. We will be part of the reason that guarantees that the whole universe will finally and eternally be secure from all rebellion.

Being part of that answer is the most practical thing a human being can do. We are sought for by God's kingdom as witnesses for His character. Nothing is more meaningful than this aspect of *LGT*.

Discussion Questions

1. How does the process of Reformation proceed?
2. What false teaching was ingrained in the minds of Luther and Calvin?
3. On what basis does God desire us to love Him?
4. Who is easier to love? One who condemns, or one who heals?
5. How is God seeking to show that the Healer truly heals?
6. Do we have any part in the great controversy, or are we just spectators?
7. Who is the Best Friend we ever had?

14. Decision Time for Planet Earth

In spite of past insubordination, we believe that God stands ready to work through a repentant people. He is using Seventh-day Adventists to prepare the willing for translation. No added Fundamental Belief statement is needed to teach *LGT*. When Adventists embrace the truths they now have they will become the five wise bridesmaids. Adventist truths enflamed by the transforming Spirit will produce the light that will say to the world, "Behold your God!" The character of God will be demonstrated more clearly and winsomely by the followers of Christ than ever before on Planet Earth. It will be decision time for all, everywhere.

God is Ready to Work

God is longsuffering, merciful, and patient. Over and over again, Scripture shows that He is ready to work through people who have turned from their own ways and returned to His.

During most of the history of God's people, they have been wayward. Yet He waits. He desires to provoke them to a deeper experience. It was true in the time of Israel; it was true in the time of the early church; it is true now in the time of the latter rain and the last-day church. The lonely God still waits for His distracted bride. His love is not diminished. The Bridegroom continues to stand at the altar, while His bride makes "herself ready" (Revelation 19:7, 8).

Always God is working providentially for His people. He does not leave Himself without witnesses to reveal the truth about His character. In the 19th century He raised up a movement and centered it in the Seventh-day Adventist Church. Many are the days of glory in the history of His working through her. Many also the days of humiliation for her failings.

She is battle-scarred and burnt because in her hallowed halls, for every Satanic attack launched in stealth and sophistry, defenders of truth have met word with word, steel with steel, false doctrine with true. The Lord is a Man of War (Exodus 15:3). So are His faithful believers. In ages past they contended for the faith delivered to the saints (Jude 3). Today, they contend still.

The Mission of God's People Today

The mission of the Seventh-day Adventist Church is, in God's eyes, still what it has always been—to prepare His people for translation (Ephesians 4:7-16; 5:25-27; Revelation 7:1-3, 13, 14; 19:7, 8; 14:1-5; 1 Corinthians 15:51-54). Brands are plucked from the burning (Zechariah 3:2) to become burning firebrands for truth. The war is not over (Revelation 12:17). God's own stand to their post of duty. Sound teaching has lost none of its power. Although the forest of error grows up round her, the pure doctrines of truth still unfold within her borders.

Lists of fundamental beliefs do not make us pure, even lists like this one enumerating the essential core of Last Generation Theology. We cannot be sanctified by mere words or by error. But words of truth become effectual as they are lived, as they are applied. As truth touches the life, it finds its way into our thoughts and feelings (John 17:17). Truth shapes the character.

We make no demands upon anyone. We simply state what we understand to be the implications of Adventism. We find these truths to be a help in our spiritual lives. We live them and share them with others. This is what we understand in our day to be the present state of the faith once delivered to the saints (Jude 3). This is the cutting edge. This is where truth lands at the closing of the age. This is where all roads end.

Embracing the Truth We Already Have

Something happens that has never happened before when Adventists embrace the truths they already have. Possession does not necessarily mean activation. In our Lord's parable, the owner of the field plowed it time and time again, missing the buried treasure that was his own (Matthew 13:44). As a people, we have done the same.

135

Without eyesalve (Revelation 3:18) we cannot see to find our glasses. Without the lens of truth we cannot understand the riches pertaining to life and godliness that Heaven has already opened to us (2 Peter 1:3, 4). All of us need to see more clearly our true poverty (Revelation 3:17) and our true wealth (Colossians 1:27).

In the day that we embrace the truths we already have, we will become the five wise bridesmaids (Matthew 25:1-13). The wedding was set but the Bridegroom delayed in returning. Ten bridesmaids, all church members, went out; all grew weary and slept. At midnight the call came, "The Bridegroom cometh!" In the darkness five of the bridesmaids sought to trim their lamps, only to realize that they had not enough oil. But five were wise, and although they too had faltered and slept, when word came of the Bridegroom's approach, they turned up their lamps. The five wise had enough oil. They had preserved their connection with God, and the Holy Spirit helped them to be living reflections of His truth.

The Last Push

Truths delivered to the people of God will now have the last push. Minds are opened to understand more fully the role of the Holy Spirit. Finally His people are ready to cooperate with Him; finally they are ready to live the life of Jesus. At last they are ready to be the Third Angel's

Message enfleshed. Having cut the knots of false doctrine and mild Laodicean half-gospels, these are filled with the Holy Spirit; these reflect the character of Christ fully, producing the light (Revelation 18:1) that will say to the world, "Behold your God!" (Isaiah 60:1-3; 35; 40:9).

Men and women who "would see Jesus" (John 12:21) will see His character echoed in His willing faithful. Never before (save in Jesus Himself) has the character of God been seen and heard so clearly and winsomely on Planet Earth. The planet will be startled. As earth is brought to the Sabbath test, there will stand the most compelling group of witnesses for God who have ever lived (1 John 4:8; Revelation 14:12).

The best evangelist is the presence of Christ in our words and actions. The character of God reproduced in us will bring this generation to the test. Armageddon is the finish of the contest between selflessness and selfishness.

When we allow God to finish His work in us, we will have reached perfection in a fallen nature that is still able to sin. But no longer will God's faithful even occasionally indulge self. We will always say "No" as Jesus said "No" to all temptations. To silence the last lingering question that perhaps Jesus was sinless because He was God, the final generation will prove beyond a shadow of a doubt that men and women with fallen natures can live without sinning. This final demonstration will contribute to the vindication of God's character, proving Satan wrong in all his evil allegations. The great controversy war will be at the point of conclusion!

Developing Characters for Eternity

When the disciples asked Jesus, "Lord, show us the Father, and it sufficeth us," Jesus responded, "Have I been so long time with you, and yet hast thou not known Me, Philip? He that hath seen Me hath seen the Father; and how sayest thou then, Show us the Father?" (John 14:8, 9). We are not Christ; we will never be Christ. But it is true that in the end we will have our Father's name written in our foreheads (Revelation 14:1; 15:1-3).

We will have the character of Christ (who demonstrated to us the character of our Father) perfectly reproduced in us. Surely then, when others see us, they will recognize in us the character-echo of the Father. They will be drawn to Him to give glory to Him. It will at last be true that, transformed by our Father, we, as the final harvest, can be described within our sphere as "merciful and gracious, longsuffering, and abundant in goodness and truth" (Exodus 34:6). This is not arrogance; it is simply God revealing what He can do with formerly self-centered rebels.

The surrender of the will draws the line of demarcation between the children of God, heirs of heaven, and the rebellious who refuse the great salvation. In spiritual things, no man can make up another's deficiency. Character is not transferable. "Though these three men, Noah, Daniel, and Job, were in it [the land], they should deliver but their own souls by their righteousness, saith the Lord God" (Ezekiel 14:14). No man can believe for another any more than he can breathe for another. No man can receive the Spirit for another. No man can give to another the character which is the fruit of the Spirit's working.

Whichever character we choose to develop, we will develop. It will be ours in the judgment. It will be ours at last when we come face to face with Jesus. It will not then be exchangeable (1 John 3:1, 2). Today is the day of salvation. Today is the day to walk with Christ.

Conclusion

Last Generation Theology: all end-time Christians believe some version of it. But do their end-time understandings match the inspired writings? Does each variety take in the significance of what the great controversy war is all about? When God's people sidestep the purpose of the great controversy, they end up with a "sin and live" scenario. Granted, this too is a kind of Last Generation Theology. So every believer living in the last generation holds to a theological system, whether loosely or systematically defined. The question then is: which form of **LGT** have they entrusted with their eternal destiny?

Ultimately, every issue is a test question. Do you love Jesus with all your heart? Living and giving these truths will cost something; there is a price tag. Will we be those who enable this to be the final generation?

Every time we sin it is a vote for Satan. But the very image of God is to be reproduced in humanity. The honor of God, the honor of Christ, is involved in the perfection of the character of His people. God is bringing to realization ancient promises. Only Adventists teach the close of probation; no other gospel permits that. Obeying God's commandments by the same kind of faith Jesus had will have its part in bringing us at last to the situation of sinlessness in which the pre-Fall Adam lived. And there are Enochs in this our day (Hebrews 11:5). Will you be one of them? Will I?

At the end of probationary time, God's willing believers make plain what is His character in word and behavior. Whatever the circumstances, they decidedly reject all modes of compulsion and coercion. It is the seal versus the mark and the contrast is drawn in black and white (Revelation 7; 13). Heaven has been waiting thousands of years for this hour. The seal is placed on those whom God can trust forever, people who are so settled into the truth that they will never be moved—they will forever say "Yes" to God. At last it is decision time for all, everywhere.

Let's roll.

Discussion Questions

1. Since the 19th century, what has been God's basic organized agency to give the Third Angel's Message?

2. What is the mission of the Seventh-day Adventist Church?

3. Where are the pure doctrines of truth still unfolding?

4. What demands do those who believe in *LGT* make upon the church organization?

5. Do Adventists already possess these truths? What happens when they are actually embraced?

6. Why is character non-transferable?

7. Do all Christians believe—in one form or another—in a Last Generation Theology?

8. Will I, in light of my now clearer understanding of Last Generation Theology, go with Jesus to a higher experience?

Section III

Invitation

Would you like more information about *LGT*? Then visit our website:

http://www.lastgenerationtheology.org

Also, download our weekly *LGT* podcast program, "Preparation for Liftoff."

To obtain current quantity pricing for *Cleanse and Close* and other print publications available from greatcontroversy.org, consult our online price list at:

http://www.greatcontroversy.org/gco/pri/gcopress.php

How to Use the *LGT14*

The *LGT14* can be studied with great benefit in a variety of ways. Some of these are listed below:

- **Prayer-meeting Series.** Help your local church recover its Seventh-day Adventist focus on present truth by spending 14 weeks working through the *LGT14*.

- **Two-week Personal Spiritual Renewal.** Prayerfully meditating over one section per day will take you through all 14 in exactly two weeks.

- **Small Group Studies.** Tired of small group studies that have nothing to do with present truth? The *LGT14* aggressively center on God's message for this time. Liven up your small groups with these practical and distinctive chapters. Invite those present to consider the discussion questions at the end of each chapter.

- **Preparatory Baptismal Studies.** In connection with other studies, the *LGT14* can provide core instruction for those preparing for baptism.

- **Seven-week Vespers Series.** Since the 14 points of *LGT* are arranged in seven couplets of two, if you do a Friday evening and

Sabbath evening vespers series for seven weeks, you can cover one of the seven theme categories each weekend.

- **Revival Meetings.** It could be arranged for a group of local or guest speakers to hold a series of meetings outlining the 14 points of Last Generation Theology.

- **Theology Student Survival Kit.** Sometimes those who love present truth feel isolated and alone while desiring to advocate truth on their campuses and in their theology programs. The *LGT14* can provide a rallying point for you and a group of revival-seeking students. Consider planning a weekend meeting held on or close to campus.

- **Youth Conference Theme.** An army of young people rightly trained can conquer the world with present truth. But we must have a grip on present truth at its core. The *LGT14* provide that rallying point.

Last Generation Theology in 14 Points

Anthropology

1. *Born With Weaknesses and Tendencies to Evil*

Man was designed to live, not to die; wired to succeed, not to fail. But at the Fall, his nature was dramatically disordered so that he is born with weaknesses and tendencies to evil. There is now in the fallen human organism little inclination to cause him to seek God or His righteousness.

2. *Lost Because of Personal Choices*

Men and women will be lost because of personal choices, not because of being born with disordered natures.

Merit

3. *God Takes the Initiative*

Repentance is a gift from God, who has taken the initiative to bring it within man's reach. His grace is sent out in search of us even before we realize our need.

4. *No Merit for Our Deeds*

Nothing we do in the Christian walk earns us even the slightest merit toward our salvation.

Cooperation

5. *Christ's Character Reproduced in Us*

Justification is God's way of simultaneously counting men right and making them so. In declaring a man just, God writes no fiction. The disciple's walk continues, and through the process of sanctification, the character of Christ is perfectly reproduced in us. Both justification and sanctification are the work of God and are necessary and causative for salvation.

6. *Obedience a Condition for Salvation*

Obedience is both a condition for salvation and an ongoing requirement of salvation.

Incarnation

7. *Jesus Emptied Himself and Took Our Fallen Flesh*

During His earthly sojourn, Jesus, God from eternity and still God, laid aside out of His possession certain of His powers of deity and lived as a man in fallen flesh among men in fallen flesh. He came not to our world to give the obedience of a lesser God to a greater, but as a man to obey God's Holy Law. He could have recovered those powers at any time, but for our sakes chose to live as we do.

8. *Jesus Tempted From Without and From Within*

That which Jesus has not assumed He has not healed. He took our disordered humanity and was tempted both from without and within. Capable of choosing to sin, constantly He chose not to sin. In this sense, His entire earthly life was lived as we will live once we are sealed. Even after probation has closed, His power and presence continue with His followers. Today He grants them an experience of present and complete victory over sin.

Atonement

9. *Jesus is Currently Making the Final Atonement*

Jesus' atonement was promised in Eden. With His incarnation and then death as our Substitute upon the cross, His atoning work was begun. He rose from the dead and went to heaven in A.D. 31 to represent us before the Father, who received His sacrifice for us. Through that sacrifice we can be right with God as soon as we accept His gift of forgiveness and heart cleansing. In A.D. 1844 He entered the second apartment of the heavenly sanctuary, commencing the closing phase of His atonement. Today, Jesus is making the final atonement.

10. *Cleansing in Heaven Connected to Cleansing on Earth*

Neither Luther nor the Millerite Adventists living in 1844 finished the Reformation or understood the angel messages of Revelation 14 and 18. The cleansing of the heavenly sanctuary is connected to the cleansing and purifying of lives on earth. The sanctuary is cleansed when God has a people who have become so settled into the truth that they will never again be moved to doubt Him or to disobey known duty. The torrent of sin that has needed forgiveness is dried up. Christ's presence remains with those who have chosen Him. The Holy Spirit empowers obedience even after the ministry of forgiveness is closed.

Delay and Hastening

11. *Delaying the Second Coming Through a Half-Gospel*

Jesus' Second Coming could have occurred within the generation that proclaimed the 1844 messages, but the same sins that kept ancient Israel out of the promised land have delayed the entrance of modern Israel into the heavenly Canaan. Unbelief, worldliness, unconsecration, and strife among the Lord's professed people have kept us in this world of sin and sorrow so many years.

12. *Hastening the Second Coming and Embracing the Harvest Principle*

Heaven has put it in our power by consecrated, Christ-reflecting lives to hasten Jesus' return. God will wait for the maturing of Christian character in a significant number of people as the chief condition determining those events, such as the latter rain, loud cry, sealing, and Sunday law, which affect the time when probation for the world shall close, and thus the time of the Second Coming.

Great Controversy and Decision Time

13. *Character Witnesses to the Great Healer*

More than forensic declarations only, the gospel is primarily concerned with telling the truth about God as our Best Friend. He is more concerned with our healing than with legal pronouncements. In the great controversy, His character witnesses tell the story of their deliverance.

14. *Decision Time for Planet Earth*

In spite of past insubordination, we believe that God stands ready to work through a repentant people. He is using Seventh-day Adventists to prepare the willing for translation. No added Fundamental Belief statement is needed to teach *LGT*. When Adventists embrace the truths they now have they will become the five wise bridesmaids. Adventist truths enflamed by the transforming Spirit will produce the light that will say to the world, "Behold your God!" The character of God will be demonstrated more clearly and winsomely by the followers of Christ than ever before on Planet Earth. It will be decision time for all, everywhere.

Resources

General

Douglass, Herbert E., *God At Risk*, Roseville, CA: Amazing Facts, 2005. 480 pp.

Kirkpatrick, Larry, *Cleanse and Close*, Highland, CA: GreatControversy.org, 2005. 160 pp.

Kirkpatrick, Larry, "What is the New Theology?" Pts. 1-14,
http://www.greatcontroversy.org/gco/rar/wint1.php
http://www.greatcontroversy.org/gco/rar/wint2.php
http://www.greatcontroversy.org/gco/rar/wint3.php
http://www.greatcontroversy.org/gco/rar/wint4.php
http://www.greatcontroversy.org/gco/rar/wint5.php
http://www.greatcontroversy.org/gco/rar/wint6.php
http://www.greatcontroversy.org/gco/rar/wint7.php
http://www.greatcontroversy.org/gco/rar/wint8.php
http://www.greatcontroversy.org/gco/rar/wint9.php
http://www.greatcontroversy.org/gco/rar/wint10.php
http://www.greatcontroversy.org/gco/rar/wint11.php
http://www.greatcontroversy.org/gco/rar/wint12.php
http://www.greatcontroversy.org/gco/rar/wint13.php
http://www.greatcontroversy.org/gco/rar/wint14.php

Priebe, Dennis, *Face-to-Face With the Real Gospel*, Roseville, CA: Amazing Facts, 1990. 90 pp.

Priebe, Dennis, *What is a Seventh-day Adventist?* Ukiah, CA: Orion Publishing, 1999. 34 pp.

Qualls, David, "A Response to *Ministry's 'Questions on Doctrine,* Then and Now' " http://www.greatcontroversy.org/reportandreview/qua-qod-whidden.php3

White, Ellen G., *The Great Controversy*, Boise, ID: Pacific Press Pub. Assn., 1911. 686 pp.

Anthropology

Kirkpatrick, Larry, "Is Our Nature Condemned?" http://www.lastgenerationtheology.org/lgt/doc/ant/kir-ionc.php

Paulson, Kevin D., "Sinners by Choice" http://www.greatcontroversy.org/reportandreview/pau-sinners.php3

Merit

Douglass, Herbert E., *Should We Ever Say, "I Am Saved"?* Boise, ID: Pacific Press Pub. Assn., 2002. 312 pp.

Maddox, Randy, *Responsible Grace: John Wesley's Practical Theology*, Nashville, TN: Kingswood Press, Abingdon Books, 1994. 416 pp.

Waggoner, E. J., *Christ Our Righteousness*, Brushton, NY: Teach Services, 2005. 138 pp.

Waggoner, E. J., *Waggoner on Romans*, Berrien Springs, MI: 1888 Message Study Committee, 1997. 226 pp.

Cooperation

Douglass, Herbert E., *The Faith of Jesus*, Brushton, NY: Teach Services, 2002. 56 pp.

Kirkpatrick, Larry, *Real Grace for Real People*, Ukiah, CA: Orion Publishing, 2003. 148 pp.

Incarnation

Crews, Joe, *Christ's Humanity*, Roseville, CA: Amazing Facts, 1984. 32 pp.

Douglass, Herbert E., *How Seventh-day Adventists Missed the Opportunity of the Century*, Highland, CA: GreatControversy.org, 2005. 48 pp.

Jones, Alonzo T., *The Consecrated Way to Christian Perfection*, Boise, ID: Pacific Press Pub. Assn., 1988. 92 pp.

Larson, Ralph, *The Word Was Made Flesh*, Cherry Valley, CA: Cherrystone Press, 1995. 365 pp.

Qualls, David, "Book Review: *Touched With Our Feelings*" http://www.greatcontroversy.org/gco/rar/qua-zurcher.php

Zurcher, J. R., *Touched With Our Feelings*, Hagerstown, MD: Review and Herald Pub. Assn., 1999. 308 pp.

Atonement

Andreasen, M. L., *The Sanctuary Service*, Hagerstown, MD: Review and Herald Pub. Assn., 1937. 311 pp.

Kirkpatrick, Larry, "Walter Martin's Trump Card" http://www.greatcontroversy.org/reportandreview/kir-qod-atonement.php3

Delay and Hastening

Douglass, Herbert E., *Why Jesus Waits*, Boise, ID: Pacific Press Pub. Assn., 2001. 96 pp.

General Conference of Seventh-day Adventists, *1973 and 1974 Annual Council Appeals*, Highland, CA: GreatControversy.org, 2005. 34 pp.

Kirkpatrick, Larry, "The Long Way Home" http://www.greatcontroversy.org/gco/ser/kir-longwayhome.php

Kirkpatrick, Larry, "Why 2K?"
    http://www.greatcontroversy.org/documents/
    sermons/sermonsLK/kir-y2k.html

Great Controversy and Decision Time

Douglass, Herbert E., *The End*, Brushton, NY:
    Teach Services, 2001. 192 pp.

Colophon

Cleanse and Close is published by
GreatControversy.org located on the internet at:

http://www.GreatControversy.org

Mission Statement
GreatControversy.org (GCO) promotes and
defends the Third Angel's Message of Revelation
14 by publishing and presenting present truth on
the internet, in print, in seminars and convoca-
tions, and by other means. We seek to meet the
challenge presented by those winds of doctrine
that, left unaddressed, would strip away our distinctive, God-given Seventh-day Adventist identity and prophetic calling. In place of weak and
watery substitutes, we present Heaven's message
of authentic victory over sin in this life and the
preparation of a people hastening the coming of
Jesus Christ.

Goals
- To uplift Jesus Christ with His forgiving, con-
  verting, healing power as the only answer
  for all the woes of mankind.

- To champion the preeminence of present truth in the Seventh-day Adventist Church.
- To stand in defense of the distinctive truths, prophetic message, and lifestyle entrusted to the Seventh-day Adventist Church, as set forth in Scripture and the Spirit of Prophecy.
- To promote, in an appropriate and responsible manner, accountability on the part of the leadership of the Seventh-day Adventist Church.
- To publish a variety of items, often with a focus on in-depth analyses, aiding church members in giving the Third Angel's Message in word and action.
- To maintain available to the public a limited selection of books and pamphlets for sale with specific reference to religious issues of interest to Christians.
- To make freely available a variety of helpful resources via the internet.
- To facilitate networking among those likewise concerned with reference to the challenges faced by the Seventh-day Adventist Church, and who wish to actively contribute to the meeting of those challenges.
- To conduct research on theological topics as they relate to Seventh-day Adventism.

- To persist in being in support of the Seventh-day Adventist Church without compromising truth for error.

Resources
Websites Operated by GCO:

    http://www.LastGenerationTheology.org

    http://www.GreatControversy.org (English Language)

    http://www.GranConflicto.org (Spanish Language)

    http://www.GreatControversy.or.kr (Korean Language)

    http://www.CollisionWithProphecy.org

    http://www.IASM.info

Books and Booklets Published by GCO:

Real Grace for Real People, by Larry Kirkpatrick

Cleanse and Close, by Larry Kirkpatrick

1973-1974 Annual Council Appeals, by General Conference of Seventh-day Adventists

How Seventh-day Adventists Missed the Opportunity of the Century, by Herbert E. Douglass

Donations

GreatControversy.org neither solicits nor accepts tithe funds. All are urged to support the

Seventh-day Adventist Church both locally and globally by the returning of tithes and offerings through the church organization. We are a non-profit corporation in the 501(c)(3) classification. Your tax-deductible gift could materially advance the fulfillment of the mission above. Thank you for considering GreatControversy.org among your giving options.

Contact Information

Physical address:
GreatControversy.org
PO Box 188
Highland, CA 92346

E-mail address:
contact@GreatControversy.org